D0983411

# GREEN Cleaning

## Natural Hints and Tips For the Eco-Friendly Household

# GREEN Cleaning

## Natural Hints and Tips For the Eco-Friendly Household

MARGARET BRIGGS
AND VIVIAN HEAD

Abbeydale Press

This edition printed in 2009



Produced by Omnipress Limited, UK
Illustrations by Tegan Sharrard
Cover design by Omnipress Limited, UK

Published by Abbeydale Press
An imprint of Bookmart Ltd
Registered number 2372865
Trading as Bookmart Ltd
Blaby Road, Wigston
Leicester LE18 4SE
England

ISBN: 978-1-86147-316-5

Printed and bound in Dubai

3 5 7 9 10 8 6 4

Some material in this book has been previously published in Vinegar—*1001 Practical Uses, Salt—the Essential Mineral and its Medicinal Benefits* and *Baking Soda—A Very Versatile Natural Substance*

**DISCLAIMER**

These ideas are passed on in good faith but the authors do not guarantee, nor cannot be held responsible, for any adverse results.

# CONTENTS

Introduction 7

VINEGAR 9
Introduction 10
A short history of vinegar 11
Green cleaning solutions with vinegar 17
- Green laundry uses 18
- Green outdoor uses 25
- Green indoor uses 31
- In the green kitchen 32
- Green cleaning solutions 37
- Further green cleaning solutions 38
- Green air fresheners and odor control 42
- Home decorating and renovating 45
- Miscellaneous green uses 50

BAKING SODA 55
Introduction 56
Green applications of baking soda 60
Glossary 63
Uses of baking soda throughout history 67
- Natron 67
- Natron and glass-making 68
- Pearlash 71
- Saleratus 72
- Developments in leavening and baking 72
- Mineral and carbonated drinks 73
- Soap 75
- Commercial production of baking soda 76

Green cleaning solutions with baking soda 79
- Green kitchen uses 81
- Green bathroom uses 90
- General green uses 94
- Green laundry uses 98
- Green outdoor uses 101
- Pets and pests 106
- Neutralizing nasty smells 108
- Miscellaneous green uses 113

LEMONS 119
Why use lemons? 120
Varieties of lemons 122
The useful lemon 124
Green cleaning solutions with lemons 125
- Green kitchen uses 126
- In the bathroom 130
- In the laundry 133
- General green cleaning 134
- Pests and pets 138
- Miscellaneous green uses 139

SALT 143
Salt in our lives 144
Green cleaning solutions with salt 145
- General green cleaning uses 146
- Pest prevention 151
- Miscellaneous green uses 152

OTHER GREEN ALTERNATIVES 155
Tea tree oil 156
Borax 158

# Introduction

Someone once asked me, is it really true that you can clean your house just by using simple ingredients such as lemons, baking soda, vinegar, and water? The simple answer is YES—and very efficiently, too.

If you believe your home is a safe place, away from pollution, I am about to disappoint you. Did you know that the levels of pollutants in indoor air can be from two to more than 100 times higher than outdoors. This is due, in part, to the products we use to clean our homes.

As more and more chemicals hit the shelves of our supermarkets claiming to be a miracle cleaner, those of us who are conscious of the environment are turning more and more to "green" cleaning. Green cleaning is just a new name for an old way of cleaning and often uses cleaners that are already on your kitchen shelves. Very often these recipes have been handed down through the generations and are just as efficient—if not more so—at eliminating that nasty stain or odor. Green cleaning is just a different way of thinking about what you put on the surfaces in your home, what you breathe in, and what you touch.

I have many friends and relatives who have complained of skin or breathing problems and violent headaches, and were convinced that it was due to the products they were using in their home. Research has also shown that babies under six months of age suffer 30 percent more ear infections and 22 percent higher risk of diarrhea. My friends were desperate to change their lifestyle but didn't want to make a lot of extra work for themselves. Although some green cleaners might not work as fast as toxic chemicals, such as bleach, it is worth asking yourself: "Are my cleaners polluting the atmosphere and damaging the ecology?"

Why use artificial air fresheners, which can provoke all kinds of unpleasant reactions, when a lemon cut in half can leave your room smelling fresh and sweet. Make sure, when the weather allows, that you open a window and let the pollutants out. Provided you do not suffer from hay fever, you can also fragrance a room by placing a vase of flowers on the table, providing a lovely natural scent.

Instead of being taken in by all the advertising slogans, why not start making your own cleaning products with the help of this book. If you find that task too daunting, then please at least make the effort to read the labels before buying a cleaning product. Look for eco-friendly ingredients such as grain alcohol instead of toxic butyl cellosolve as a solvent; coconut or other plant oils rather than petroleum as detergents; and plant-oil disinfectants such as eucalyptus, rosemary, or sage, rather than triclosan. We tend to purchase those items that we believe are the best value for money; very often these items are the ones that contain the most pollutants.

So go on, roll up your sleeves, and get cleaning the natural way! Hopefully this book will give you all the information and tips you require to make your home a much "greener" and safer place. It is also worth remembering that your home is not a hospital, and does not mean you have to kill 100 percent of germs. Just because you can't smell a cleaning product in your home, it doesn't mean that your home isn't clean. Learn more about why green cleaning products are just as effective as conventional ones, and why the fragrances used can actually be harmful to your health.

# VINEGAR

# INTRODUCTION

## NATURAL ALCHEMY

It's amazing that a product discovered by accident more than 10,000 years ago is still used so widely today—and for such a wide range of purposes. Anyone who has ever left a bottle of wine uncorked (with wine still in it) will know what happens. That's not a problem for some of us, because wine bottles are emptied promptly! However, under the effects of bacteria, the alcohol is turned into acetic acid, better known as vinegar. Even Louis Pasteur has a place in the story. His invention of pasteurization of milk came about indirectly, after he was employed by the wine-making industry to find out why wine turned bad so quickly.

Look in any Victorian household management book, for example, the works of Mrs. Beeton, and you will see endless recipes for flavored vinegars, as well as a dazzling array of applications in cleaning, laundry, and home medicine.

As recently as World War I, vinegar was being used to treat wounds. Today, it is recommended for treatment of rashes, bites, and other minor ailments.

Throughout history there have been countless civilizations that have been aware of the wide ranging benefits of vinegar to the palate, to hygiene, and to the pocket. Here is a staple from your pantry shelf—economical, always on hand, ready to serve in a variety of ways. One bottle of white distilled vinegar contains a whole shelf's worth of specialized cleaners.

This chapter provides a short summary of vinegar through the ages and differences from other cultures. It also gives a comprehensive list of the many practical and money-saving hints and tips that you may find invaluable around the home.

# A SHORT HISTORY OF VINEGAR

Ancient civilizations were quick to recognize the versatility of vinegar. The Babylonians used it as a preservative and Roman legionnaires used it as a beverage. Cleopatra demonstrated its solvent properties to win a bet, Hippocrates extolled its medicinal qualities, and when Hannibal crossed the Alps, it was vinegar that helped pave the way. Was vinegar the world's first bulldozer?

**EARLY MULTIPURPOSE PANACEA**

Vinegar has a 10,000 year history, dating from the production of alcoholic drinks—beer, wine, and other spirits. Vinegar is a natural by-product of alcoholic beverages and its discovery was almost certainly accidental. People made the discovery in different parts of the world independently, and for as long as there have been undistilled, alcoholic drinks, there has been vinegar. Ancient civilizations as far back as the Sumerians used vinegar as a condiment, a preservative, a medicine, an antibiotic, and a detergent, just as we do today.

**BABYLONIAN BEVERAGE**

The earliest written record is 5000 BC, when the Babylonians made vinegar by fermenting the fruit of date palms. An old Babylonian saying that "Beer that went sour wandered into the kitchen" suggests that these early people used vinegar when cooking.

**RELIGIOUS REFERENCES**

Vinegar is mentioned in the Bible, in both the Old and New Testaments—in the Book of Ruth and in Proverbs. It is also specifically called for in the making of haroseth in Pesachim, a section of the Talmud, the Jewish book of civil and ceremonial law.

**ROMAN REFRESHMENT**

The word "vinegar" comes from the Latin word *vinum*,

meaning "wine" and *acer* meaning "sour." The French word, *vinaigre* derives from Latin. The word *alegar* was used for vinegar made from ale or beer. The Romans made vinegar from grapes, figs, dates, and rye. The armies of Julius Caesar would drink Posca, a refreshing mixture of water and vinegar, as part of every meal and for its antiseptic properties.

### PHILOSOPHICAL PANACEA

Hippocrates, the father of medicine, prescribed the drinking of vinegar for his patients in ancient Greece. Many ancient cultures used vinegar and valued it for its medicinal benefits. Aristotle and Sophocles also made reference to uses of vinegar.

### MOLEHILLS FROM MOUNTAINS

Without vinegar, Hannibal's march over the Alps to Rome may not have been possible. The chronicles of Livy describing this historic march include the essential role vinegar played in the task of getting Hannibal's elephants over perilous mountain trails.

Frequently, the passes across the Alps were too narrow for the huge elephants. Hannibal's solution was to cut branches and stack them around the boulders that blocked their way. Soldiers then set the wood on fire. When the rocks were good and hot, vinegar was poured onto them, turning the stones soft and crumbly. The soldiers could then chip the rocks away, making a passage for both the troops and elephants.

### EGYPTIAN ENIGMA

Many paintings discovered in Egyptian burial tombs from the 11th and 13th dynasty show people busy brewing. Legend has it that Cleopatra made her own entry into the vinegar history book by making a wager with Anthony that she could consume a meal worth a million sesterces, which represented a huge amount of wealth.

How did she go about winning her bet? At the start of the banquet, she placed a valuable pearl in a vase filled with vinegar, then at the end of the meal she drank the liquid in which the pearl had dissolved! Sadly, the act did her no good because she was arrested soon after and stripped of all her assets.

**CRYPTEX CRACKER**

Leonardo da Vinci knew about the effects of vinegar on papyrus and invented an ingenious mechanical device to allow secret, coded messages to be sent without being read if intercepted. In his novel, entitled *The Da Vinci Code*, Dan Brown uses Leonardo's cryptex idea to hide a map around a phial of vinegar. If the phial broke, the vinegar would dissolve the papyrus and the information written on it.

**ALL KINDS OF ALCHEMY**

Alchemists were interested in vinegar from early times and the vinegar makers jealously guarded their manufacturing secrets. For centuries, the first concern was to accelerate its production, and there were so many recipes that the vinegar makers remarked that living material accelerated the acidification. From then on anything was possible: vine shoots, brambles, vegetables, even fish tongues were thrown into the wine!

**CHINESE CHENCU**

Meanwhile, in China a different form of vinegar was developed from rice water. Chencu, or mature vinegar, has been used as a kind of flavoring for more than 1,000 years.

Further documentary proof confirms Modena as the birthplace of balsamic vinegar, whose method of preparation did not undergo any significant changes for many centuries. The traditional raw material for balsamic vinegar had always been wine vinegar, which was aged for hundreds of years. In 1861 Mr. Aggazzotti, a lawyer, introduced a revolutionary production technique that used concentrated grape must as the raw material instead of wine vinegar. This is the method that has been used ever since to produce traditional balsamic vinegars.

### VINEGAR MAKERS WORTH THEIR SALT

From the reign of Charles VI, the occupation of vinegar distilling was made into a corporation, which was first registered in October 1394, in Paris. The statutes were completed in 1514, making up a trade body under the official title of "Vinegar makers, mustard and sauce-makers, brandy liqueur and rectified spirit distillers." Workers in this trade had to be "sound in limb and clean in dress."

### PLAGUE POTION

During the Middle Ages, vinegar was heavily used, not only as a drink and condiment, but also for washing and for treating many illnesses, such as the plague, leprosy, fever, and snake bites. Because fear and chaos reigned during these plagues, people performed odd and cruel rituals to spare their town.

In some towns and villages in England, there are still the old market crosses that have a depression at the foot of the stone cross. This was filled with vinegar during times of plague, because it was believed that vinegar would kill any germs on the coins handled by the victims and so contain the disease.

### FOUR THIEVES

Legends also abounded about those who survived, in particular, four thieves who robbed the bodies and houses of the dead but did not contract the illness. The legend places the thieves in Marseilles, or Toulouse, or perhaps London, during the plague epidemic that ravaged Europe during the 17th and 18th centuries. In 1628, 1632, or 1722, they were caught and sentenced to death, but were told they would be spared if they revealed the secret for their survival: the Vinegar of Four Thieves.

Some recipes called for red wine vinegar, others for cider vinegar, mixed with herbs-lavender blossoms, rue, rosemary, sage; some added wormwood, thyme, mint, and garlic, and the vinegar was either steeped in the sun or buried in a crock. The unfortunate victims thought that they could get immunity by drinking it, sniffing it, or splashing it on the body. Despite the fact that it had long been proven not to confer any immunity, the Vinegar of Four Thieves was used as late as 1793, when yellow fever hit Philadelphia.

## THE WORLD IN A COUPLE OF SHAKES

As explorers began to travel the world's seas, vinegar became a vital ingredient of food preservation, and it's likely that the New Worlds would not have been discovered as quickly without it.

## COMMERCIAL BREAK

The Industrial Revolution started a change in the commercial production of vinegar. The distillation of wood was used to produce acetic acid (the main ingredient of vinegar). After dilution and coloring with caramel or burned sugar it was sold to an unsuspecting public as the real thing.

## PASTEUR'S PUBLICATION

Despite the most far fetched theories proferred to explain the process of successful alcohol production, everyone agreed that a certain temperature and air were fundamental ingredients. But nobody discovered the reason for the formation of a veil on the surface of wine until Louis Pasteur published the most modern scientific research on vinegar, still used as a reference today. It was in 1865 that Pasteur solved the mystery surrounding vinegar. He had been asked to identify methods of keeping wine and vinegar, both commodities of great importance in France, in top condition, without deterioration during production, storage, and transport. His work and treatment method became known as pasteurization, and were later applied to milk.

It was this research that brought about the process for commercial production of vinegar.

## VICTORIAN CONTRACEPTIVES

Like lemons, vinegar was also used as a cheap yet somewhat unreliable contraceptive by the prostitutes of Victorian times.

# Green Cleaning Solutions with Vinegar

## GREEN LAUNDRY USES

CLEANING AND REFRESHING AN IRONING BOARD..........19
CLEANING THE BOTTOM OF AN IRON........................19
COLLARS AND CUFFS ..........................................19
COLORS ......................................................20
DEODORIZE A WOOL SWEATER................................20
DELICATES....................................................20
DYEING .......................................................20
FABRIC SOFTENER AND STATIC CLING REDUCER ..........20
GETTING RID OF SHINY MARKS WHEN IRONING............20
GETTING RID OF UNDERARM MARKS .......................20
LEATHER.......................................................21
LINT ON CLOTHING ............................................21
LABEL REMOVER ..............................................21
NEW CLOTHES .................................................21
PREVENTING COLORS FROM RUNNING .....................21
PREVENTING FADING OF COLORED
TOWELS AND QUILTS ........................................21
REMOVING COLA STAINS ......................................21
REMOVING GREASE FROM SUEDE ...........................22
REMOVING OR SETTING CREASES ...........................22
REMOVING STIFFNESS FROM NEW JEANS...................22
REMOVING TAR FROM JEANS.................................22
REMOVING THE SMELL OF BLEACH .........................22
REMOVING THE SMELL OF SMOKE FROM CLOTHES ........22
REMOVING WHITE MARKS WHEN LETTING HEMS DOWN ..22
SILK ...........................................................23
SOFT FLUFFY BLANKETS ......................................23
STAIN REMOVER ...............................................23
STATIC CLING..................................................23
STEAM IRON CLEANER..........................................23
TERRY DIAPERS 1 AND 2 ......................................23
TERRY DIAPERS 3 .............................................24

Use only white vinegar for the following tips and applications.

### CLEANING AND REFRESHING AN IRONING BOARD

Spritz the ironing board cover to freshen it up and iron while it is still damp. This is cheaper than any purchased fabric freshener or odor eliminator.

### CLEANING THE BOTTOM OF AN IRON

Use a paste of vinegar and baking soda to clean the sole plate of your iron. It will be smooth, clean, and shiny and will not harm any surface.

### COLLARS AND CUFFS

Collars and cuffs can be cleaned by rubbing a thick paste of baking soda and vinegar onto the stains before washing in the usual way.

## COLORS

Any colored clothing item that has become dulled can be brightened by soaking it in 1 gallon (3.75 liters) warm water and 1 cup (225 ml) vinegar. Follow this with a clear water rinse.

## DEODORIZE A WOOL SWEATER

Wash the sweater, then rinse in equal parts of vinegar and water to remove odors.

## DELICATES

If you are washing delicate items by hand, follow the garment's care instruction, but add 1 or 2 tablespoons of vinegar to the last rinse to help remove soap residue.

## DYEING

When dyeing fabric, include 1 cup (225 ml) white vinegar in a hot dye bath to set the color.

## FABRIC SOFTENER AND STATIC CLING REDUCER

Use as you would a liquid fabric softener.

## GETTING RID OF SHINY MARKS WHEN IRONING

Mix half vinegar and half water and put into a spritzer bottle. When ironing, use the spray to help remove iron-made creases or shiny areas in the fabric. Spritz a shirt for a clean, odor-free, crisp garment, especially collars and underarm areas. Use a damp cloth and gently rub shiny areas, such as those that appear when the iron is too hot and you iron over a zipper, then repress and the shine will be gone. Repeat if necessary.

## GETTING RID OF UNDERARM MARKS

Perspiration marks can be eliminated by soaking them with vinegar before laundering in the usual way. To remove the solid residue on the underarm of a shirt left by deodorants, soak the area in white vinegar until saturated, then wash as usual. This removes any odor as well.

### LEATHER

Clean leather with a mixture of 2⁄3 cup (150 ml) boiled linseed oil and 2⁄3 cup (150 ml) vinegar. Carefully apply to any spots with a soft cloth and let dry.

### LINT ON CLOTHING

Another reason to use vinegar in the rinse cycle is that it cuts down on the lint. Put 2⁄3–1 cup (150–225 ml) in the rinse cycle. You will notice the reduction in lint on the family's clothes.

### LABEL REMOVER

Soak the label or sticker with vinegar, let stand until it is saturated, then peel off.

### NEW CLOTHES

Some new clothes may be treated with a chemical that can be irritating to sensitive skin. Soak new clothing in 1 gallon (3.75 liters) of water with 1 cup (225 ml) of vinegar. Rinse, then wash as usual.

### PREVENTING COLORS FROM RUNNING

Use white vinegar if washing something that will bleed. Pour some white vinegar in the washing machine, fill with cold water, and then add soap and clothes.

### PREVENTING FADING OF COLORED TOWELS AND QUILTS

Add 2⁄3 cup (150 ml) of vinegar to the laundry to prevent fading. Handmade quilts can be soaked in lots of cold water using 1 cup (225 ml) of vinegar on the first time of washing.

### REMOVING COLA STAINS

Remove spots caused by cola-based soft drinks from 100 percent cotton, and cotton-polyester fabrics. Sponge distilled vinegar directly onto the stain and rub away the spots, then clean according to the directions on the manufacturer's label. This must be done within 24 hours of the spill.

## REMOVING GREASE FROM SUEDE

Dip a toothbrush in vinegar and gently brush over the grease spot.

## REMOVING OR SETTING CREASES

For setting creases and also removing them when in the wrong place, iron with a pressing cloth soaked in a solution of 1 part vinegar to 2 parts water. This is a strong, smelly solution, so use in a well-ventilated room. The smell will soon leave the garment after airing.

## REMOVING STIFFNESS FROM NEW JEANS

Wash jeans for the first time by turning them inside out and adding 1 cup (225 ml) of vinegar to the wash. It takes the stiffness out of new jeans.

## REMOVING TAR FROM JEANS

Pour a few drops of vinegar on the stains, then put them in the washing machine and wash as normal.

## REMOVING THE SMELL OF BLEACH

If you use bleach to remove stains or to whiten cotton, remove the bleach smell by adding 1 cup (225 ml) of vinegar to the final rinse.

## REMOVING THE SMELL OF SMOKE FROM CLOTHES

Get the stale cigarette smoke smell out of clothes by adding 1 cup (225 ml) of vinegar to a bath of hot water. Hang the clothes above the steam. Leave them in the bathroom overnight, with a window open if possible.

## REMOVING WHITE MARKS WHEN LETTING HEMS DOWN

When you let hems down on children's clothes, such as skirts and dresses, there is often a white mark where the fabric was turned up. Warm up your iron, and with an old toothbrush dipped in a little vinegar diluted with a small amount of water, scrub the mark and press. It usually comes right out. If not, then repeat.

SILK
Dip silks (but do not soak) in a mixture of $^{2}/_{3}$ cup (150 ml) mild detergent, 2 tablespoons of vinegar, and $3^{1}/_{2}$ cups (900 ml) of water. Rinse well, then roll in a heavy towel to soak up the excess moisture. Iron while still damp.

SOFT FLUFFY BLANKETS
Adding $2^{1}/_{2}$ cups (570 ml) of white vinegar to a bathtub of water will make a good rinse for both cotton and wool blankets and leaves them free of soap, with their nap as soft and fluffy as new.

STAIN REMOVER
For stains caused by grass, coffee, tea, fruits and berries, mildew and ink, soak clothing in full strength vinegar.

STATIC CLING
A good way to control static cling is to add $^{2}/_{3}$–1 cup (150–225 ml) of vinegar to the last rinse cycle of your wash.

STEAM IRON CLEANER
Mineral deposits may be removed from an old steam iron by filling it with a solution of equal parts white vinegar and water and letting it steam until dry. Rinse the tank with clean water, refill it, and shake water through the steam holes over an old piece of material. Test on an old cloth before ironing. It is not advisable to try this on a new iron because the acidity of the vinegar may damage the iron.

TERRY DIAPERS 1
Use 1 cup (225 ml) of vinegar in 7.5 liters of water in the diaper bucket to neutralize the urine in cloth diapers. It also helps to keep them from staining.

TERRY DIAPERS 2
Adding 1 cup (225 ml) vinegar during the rinse cycle equalizes the pH balance and has been reported to prevent diaper rash.

## TERRY DIAPERS 3

Using vinegar in the wash cycle cuts the cost. Use half the recommended detergent during the wash and skip the fabric softener. Instead, put the diapers through an additional rinse at the end.

## GREEN OUTDOOR USES

AZALEAS ........................................................ 26
CHROME POLISH ............................................... 26
CLEANING WINDOWS .......................................... 26
CLEANING WINDSHIELD AND KEEPING ICE OFF ........... 26
DISCOURAGING ANTS .......................................... 26
DISSOLVE CHEWING GUM ................................... 26
DRAIN CLEANER ................................................ 27
GETTING RID OF SLUGS ..................................... 27
GRASS/WEED KILLER .......................................... 27
INCREASE SOIL ACIDITY ..................................... 27
INSTANT ANTIBACTERIAL AID FOR GARDENERS
OR RAMBLERS ................................................ 27
KEEPING CATS AWAY ......................................... 28
KEEPING FLIES FROM A SWIMMING POOL ................. 28
LAWNS WITH NO BROWN PATCHES .......................... 28
NEUTRALIZE GARDEN LIME .................................. 28
PROLONGING THE LIFE OF PLANTS ....................... 28
REPELLING MOSQUITOES .................................... 28
REMOVING CALCIUM BUILDUP FROM BRICKWORK ........ 28
REMOVING DIESEL SMELLS .................................. 28
REMOVING LIME DEPOSITS FROM WINDSHIELD JETS ...... 29
REMOVING PAINT FROM GLASS ............................. 29
REMOVING RUST FROM BOLTS, SCREWS, NAILS,
AND HINGES .................................................. 29
REMOVING STAINS FROM FLOWERPOTS ................... 29
RIPENING MELONS WITHOUT MOLD ....................... 29
SEPTIC TANK USERS .......................................... 29
STAINS ON CONCRETE ........................................ 29
VINEGAR AS A WEED SUPPRESSANT ....................... 29
WEED SUPPRESSANT II ....................................... 30
WOOD STAIN .................................................... 30

The uses of vinegar need not be limited to indoors; there are plenty of areas outside that need its help as well.

## AZALEAS

Pour vinegar over your azaleas to give a sheen over the leaves.

## CHROME POLISH

Apply full-strength vinegar to a cloth to polish the chrome on your car.

## CLEANING WINDOWS

Clean windows with a solution of 2 tablespoons of vinegar to 4 cups (1 liter) of warm water. Wash from top to bottom on the inside of windows and from side to side on the outside. This way you will be able to tell on which side any smears are.

Using dry newspaper instead of a cloth to polish with is an old trick as well.

Keep a solution of 50/50 white vinegar and water in a spray bottle to use for removing spots from windows.

## CLEANING WINDSHIELDS AND KEEPING ICE OFF

If you have to leave your car outside overnight in the winter, mix 3 parts vinegar to 1 part water and coat the windows with this solution. This vinegar- and water-combination will keep windshields ice and frost-free.

## DISCOURAGING ANTS

If you have problems with ants and other insects invading your home, they are probably crossing your doorways and windowsills. If you pour vinegar across the opening sill, it stops them from crossing.

## DISSOLVE CHEWING GUM

Saturate the area with vinegar. If the vinegar is heated, it will work faster.

## DRAIN CLEANER

Vinegar and baking soda cause a chemical reaction when combined, so be prepared. They break down fatty acids from grease, other foods, and a buildup of soap into simpler substances.

Pour 1/4 cup (2 oz) of baking soda and 2/3 cup (150 ml) of vinegar into the drain. Cover, if possible, while the solution fizzes. Follow this with a bucketful of very hot water.

## GETTING RID OF SLUGS

If you have a slug problem, drop a few drops of white vinegar on them. Be careful not to get the vinegar on your plants.

## GRASS/WEED KILLER

Kill weeds or unwanted grass with direct application of vinegar onto the trouble spot.

## INCREASE SOIL ACIDITY

In hard water areas, add a 1 cup (225 ml) of vinegar to 1 gallon (3.75 liters) of tap water for watering acid-loving plants such as rhododendrons, heathers, or azaleas. The vinegar will release iron in the soil for the plants to use.

Azaleas will benefit from an occasional watering with a mixture of two tablespoons of vinegar to a 4 cups (1 liter) of water.

## INSTANT ANTIBACTERIAL AID FOR GARDENERS OR RAMBLERS

If you hate to wear gloves when gardening (except, of course, when working with roses, blackberries, or thistles) you will, once in a while, get nicked or scratched. White vinegar can be used to treat such scratches if you are not near a water supply. This stings for a second or two, but saves a long trek to the tap.

### KEEPING CATS AWAY

Pour vinegar around the children's sand box to keep cats from using it as their litter box. Reapply about every two months just to be sure. Also you can sprinkle a little vinegar on your garden paths and patios to help keep cats away.

### KEEPING FLIES FROM A SWIMMING POOL

Pour vinegar around the sides of your pool and it helps keeps flies away.

### LAWNS WITH NO BROWN PATCHES

Put a tablespoon of vinegar in your dog's drinking water every day and you will no longer have those brown spots in your lawn from the dog's urine.

### NEUTRALIZE GARDEN LIME

Rinse your hands liberally with vinegar after working with garden lime to avoid rough and flaking skin.

### PROLONGING THE LIFE OF PLANTS

Pour a mixture of vinegar and water over household plants and bouquets to prolong their lifespan.

### REPELLING MOSQUITOES

Add a tablespoonful of apple cider vinegar to a quart of drinking water. This helps to deal with heat stress and also helps to repel mosquitoes.

### REMOVING CALCIUM BUILDUP FROM BRICKWORK

To get rid of calcium buildup on brick or on limestone, use a spray bottle with half vinegar and half water, then just let it set. The solution will do all the work.

### REMOVING DIESEL SMELLS

If you have the misfortune to spill diesel fuel either on clothes or yourself, you will know that the smell is horrible and refuses to go away. A little vinegar added to the washing machine will take most, if not all, of the smell out.

### REMOVING LIME DEPOSITS FROM WINDSHIELD JETS

Use full-strength vinegar on a rag to wipe away the lime deposits left on your car's paint, windows, and windshield jets.

### REMOVING PAINT FROM GLASS

Hot vinegar can be used to remove paint from glass. This works well around windows where you've accidentally got paint on the glass. Just heat up vinegar and use a cloth to wipe away the paint.

### REMOVING RUST FROM BOLTS, SCREWS, NAILS, AND HINGES

To remove rust from bolts and other metals, soak them in full-strength vinegar. Put the metal objects in a container and cover with vinegar. Seal the container and shake. Let it stand overnight. Dry the objects to prevent corrosion.

### REMOVING STAINS FROM FLOWERPOTS

That staining that occurs in clay and plastic flowerpots and their saucers comes right out without scrubbing. Just fill the kitchen sink with cold water and add plain white vinegar about ⅔ water to ⅓ vinegar. Soak the pots and saucers until they look clean and new. This may take up to an hour. Wash with soap and water before reusing.

### RIPENING MELONS WITHOUT MOLD

Try rubbing each melon with about a teaspoonful of full-strength vinegar every few days as they begin to ripen.

### SEPTIC TANK USERS

If you have a septic tank, use vinegar instead of harsh chemicals to clean the toilet bowl. Leave overnight if you can. It will help to keep the germs down.

### STAINS ON CONCRETE

Remove unsightly marks on concrete by applying vinegar directly to the stain.

## VINEGAR AS A WEED SUPPRESSANT

Mix 3 parts water with 1 part concentrated acetic acid, or vinegar, to get a final concentration of 6 percent. You should be able to achieve a 6 percent acetic acid concentration by mixing household table vinegar with concentrated lemon or lime juice in equal parts.

This will act on the young tender new growth of plants. It is not taken into the roots but basically burns the top growth. If repeated consistently every week to 10 days during the vigorous growing season, it will eventually kill off the plants by starving the roots.

Please note that this is a suppressant for hardier perennial weeds, not a weed killer.

It may be effective on young annual plants and should help control perennials with multiple applications.

## WEED SUPPRESSANT II

Kill individual weeds by pouring hot vinegar on.
This might take a couple of times to work completely.
I would suggest this treatment for patios and pathways, rather than lawns, or among precious herbaceous beds.

Alternatively, use white vinegar straight from the bottle to pour on the weeds and grasses that come up through the paved area. Pour on and leave for a couple of days. The weeds will die back and won't reappear for several months.

## WOOD STAIN

White vinegar can be mixed with water-base inks to make a wonderful stain for wood. The resulting finish is the color of the ink with a silvery sheen. Simply pour vinegar into a mixing jar, add the ink until the desired color is achieved, and apply to the wood with a brush or rag. Wipe off any excess and let it dry. Since the bulk of the mixture is vinegar, wood warpage is minimal.

# GREEN INDOOR USES

Vinegar is well recognized as a green cleaning and sanitizing agent. It is especially effective in removing inorganic soils and mineral deposits, such as hard water films. As a sanitizer, it is effective against a broad range of bacteria, yeasts, and molds, destroying or reducing these organisms to acceptable levels.

Additionally, vinegar has been found to be effective as a rinse agent in reducing levels of *E. coli* on various countertop surfaces (for example, laminate, wood, tile, concrete, stainless steel, and granite).

Vinegar has been used commercially to reduce micro-organisms in slaughterhouses and poultry plants; to reduce mineral and lime deposits in lavatory pipes; to prevent milk stone buildup in tanks used by the milk industry; to clean vehicles and equipment used in the construction industry; and to wash and rinse walls and ceilings in restaurants and food establishments.Cleaning with vinegar is much safer and cheaper than using commercial products and has the following additional advantages:

It's biodegradable—a mild organic acid
It's easy to dispense and control
It's safe for stainless steel, used by the food industry
It's relatively nontoxic and stable, so safe for handling
It's less likely to leave harmful residues behind
It has a pleasant, clean smell
It can be used where environmental considerations are especially important.

Once again, Mrs. Beeton and her contemporaries give insight into the many uses and applications that were known to our grandparents and great grandparents.

**Please note:** Red wine or cider vinegar should be avoided because their coloring may cause staining. White distilled vinegar is best for cleaning.

## IN THE GREEN KITCHEN

BRIGHTER STAINLESS STEEL .................................. 33
CARPET CLEANERS .................................. 33
CARPET CLEANING .................................. 33
CLEANING CUTTING BOARDS .................................. 33
CLEANING DECANTERS AND BOTTLES .................................. 34
CLEANING KETTLES .................................. 34
CLEANING OUT A COFFEEMAKER .................................. 34
CLEANING PLASTICS .................................. 34
CLEANING PLASTIC SHOWER CURTAINS .................................. 34
CLEANING THE REFRIGERATOR .................................. 34
CLEANING WASTE DISPOSAL UNITS .................................. 34
CLEANING WORK SURFACES .................................. 34
DISINFECTANT .................................. 34
GREASE CUTTER .................................. 35
LOOSENING TOUGH STAINS .................................. 35
MICROWAVE CLEANER .................................. 35
OVEN CLEANER I .................................. 35
OVEN CLEANER II .................................. 35
REFRESHING THE ICE TRAY .................................. 35
REMOVING COFFEE AND TEA STAINS .................................. 35
REMOVING FRUIT STAINS .................................. 36
REMOVING NONOILY STAINS FROM CARPETS .................................. 36
REVIVING OLD KITCHEN SPONGES .................................. 36
RINSING DISHES .................................. 36
RINSING IN THE DISHWASHER .................................. 36
SOAKING BADLY STAINED POTS AND PANS .................................. 36
NICER SMELLING BREAD BOX .................................. 36

**BRIGHTER STAINLESS STEEL**

Spots on your stainless steel or aluminum kitchen equipment can be removed by rubbing with white vinegar.

**Note:** Do not leave in vinegar, or the pots will corrode.

**CARPET CLEANERS**

The colors in carpets and rugs will often take on a new lease of life if they are brushed with a mixture of 1 cup (225 ml ) of vinegar in 1 gallon (3.75 liters) of water.

**CARPET CLEANING**

Use distilled vinegar to rinse your carpets after shampooing. The carpet will stay fresh longer and it removes any detergent residue. Use 4 tablespoons per 1 gallon (3.75 liters) of water.

**CLEANING CUTTING BOARDS**

Wipe down cutting boards with full-strength vinegar. It will clean them, cut grease, and absorb odors.

### CLEANING DECANTERS AND BOTTLES

Use 2 teaspoons of salt, moistened with vinegar. Shake well and rinse thoroughly with water.

### CLEANING KETTLES

If you get lime deposits in your kettle, gently boil $2/3$ cup (150 ml) of white vinegar with the water, then rinse well.

### CLEANING OUT A COFFEEMAKER

Fill the water reservoir halfway with vinegar and run the coffeemaker as you normally do, and then run it once full of water. The coffeemaker will be spotless.

### CLEANING PLASTICS

Plastic can be cleaned and made antistatic by wiping down with a solution of one tablespoon of distilled vinegar to 2 quarts (2 liters) of water. This should prevent dust from settling as well.

### CLEANING PLASTIC SHOWER CURTAINS

To prevent mildew on plastic shower curtains, keep a spray bottle of vinegar and water in the bathroom and use regularly.

### CLEANING THE REFRIGERATOR

Clean the refrigerator by washing with a solution of equal parts of water and vinegar.

### CLEANING WASTE DISPOSAL UNITS

Clean and freshen the waste disposal by running a tray of ice cubes through it with 6 tablespoons of vinegar poured over them once a week.

### CLEANING WORK SURFACES

Wipe all kitchen work surfaces down with full-strength white vinegar to clean them and reduce bacteria.

### DISINFECTANT

Kill germs in the bathroom by mixing vinegar and water in a spritzer bottle. Apply liberally.

### GREASE CUTTER

Vinegar is an excellent grease cutter. Boil out fat fryers every week with vinegar and water. This is very cost effective and safe, with no harsh chemicals or risk of fire. It works well on extractor hoods, too.

### LOOSENING TOUGH STAINS

To loosen hard-to-clean stains in glass or porcelain pots or pans, boil 3 tablespoons of white vinegar with 2½ cups (570 ml) of water. Wash in hot, soapy water.

### MICROWAVE CLEANER

To clean a microwave oven, all you need to do is put a couple of tablespoons of vinegar in a bowl with a cup of water. Microwave on High for 45 seconds to 1 minute (the time depends on your particular model). Carefully take the bowl out and wipe out the oven. Any baked-on splatters will be softened and easily removed.

### OVEN CLEANER I

Dampen your cleaning cloth in white vinegar and water and use it to wipe out your oven.

### OVEN CLEANER II

To keep your freshly cleaned oven from stinking up your house next time you bake something, wipe it with white vinegar poured directly on the sponge as a final rinse. It neutralizes the harsh alkali of oven cleaners.

### REFRESHING THE ICE TRAY

Boil some vinegar and let it cool for a while. Pour it, still hot, into the tray. Wait a few moments and then wipe it clean.

### REMOVING COFFEE AND TEA STAINS

An equal mixture of salt and white vinegar will clean coffee and tea stains from china cups.

## REMOVING FRUIT STAINS

To remove fruit stains from your hands, rub them with a little white vinegar and wipe with a cloth.

## REMOVING NONOILY STAINS FROM CARPETS

Apply a mixture of one teaspoon of liquid detergent and 1 teaspoon of distilled vinegar in 2½ cups (570 ml) of lukewarm water to the stain. Rub gently with a soft brush or towel. Rinse with a towel, moistened with clean water and blot dry. Repeat until the stain is gone and then dry quickly, using a fan or hair dryer. This should be done as soon as the stain is discovered.

## REVIVING OLD KITCHEN SPONGES

Renew old sponges by washing them in vinegar water, then soaking overnight in 4 cups (1 liter) of water with 3 tablespoons vinegar added to it.

## RINSING DISHES

Use white vinegar mixed with water to rinse off the dishes after washing. This will take the soap off and leave them squeaky clean. A splash of vinegar added to the rinse water will also keep glasses from water spotting.

## RINSING IN THE DISHWASHER

Pour 3 tablespoons vinegar to your dishwasher rinse cycle for streak-free, sparkling dishes every time instead of using a rinse aid.

## SOAKING BADLY STAINED POTS AND PANS

Soak non-aluminum, food-stained pots and pans in full-strength white vinegar for 30 minutes. Rinse in hot, soapy water.

## NICER SMELLING BREAD BOX

After cleaning out the bread box, keep it smelling pleasant by wiping it down with a cloth moistened in distilled vinegar. Allow to dry before replacing the bread.

# GREEN CLEANING SOLUTIONS

Vinegar cleans by cutting grease. This makes it useful for melting away gummy buildup. It also inhibits mold growth, dissolves mineral accumulations, freshens the air, kills bacteria, and slows its regrowth.

**ALL-PURPOSE WINDOW WASH**
3 tablespoons white distilled vinegar
½ teaspoon liquid soap or detergent
2½ cups (575 ml) water

Combine the ingredients in a spray bottle, and shake to blend. Spray it on, and then remove with a squeegee or paper towel. Polish with dry newspaper when dry.
The shelf life of this mix is indefinite, but make sure you keep it in a labeled bottle.

**CHEAP CLEANING SOLUTION**
⅓ part white vinegar
⅓ part rubbing alcohol
⅓ part water
3 drops dishwashing liquid

Mix this into a (recycled) spray bottle and you have the equivalent of the floor cleaner. Just spray and mop. It is also recommended for deodorizing a room and for a fast cleanup. Use this on any tile floors with great results. The alcohol is added to make it dry faster, but you could leave it out, if you want.

**FLOOR CLEANER WITH FRAGRANT HERBS**
2 tablespoons liquid soap or detergent
4–8 tablespoons white distilled vinegar
6 tablespoons fragrant herb tea (peppermint adds antibacterial qualities)

Combine ingredients in a bucket of water. Swirl the water around until it lathers a little. Proceed as normal. Discard the remainder after use.

## FURTHER GREEN CLEANING SOLUTIONS

ANTIQUE APPLIANCES ........................................ 39
BRASSWARE .................................................. 39
CARPET SPOT AND STAIN REMOVER ........................ 39
CLEANING A SHOWERHEAD ................................. 39
CLEANING A WHIRLPOOL TUB .............................. 39
CLEANING DRAINS ........................................... 39
CLEANING FIREPLACE DOORS ............................... 40
CLEANING FLUID FOR BRASS AND COPPER ................ 40
CLEANING METAL SCREENS AND ALUMINUM
FURNITURE ................................................. 40
CLEANING PORCELAIN, ENAMEL BATHS AND SINKS ...... 40
FLOOR CLEANER ............................................. 40
FURNITURE POLISH .......................................... 40
HARD WATER DEPOSITS ...................................... 40
REMOVING LIME DEPOSITS................................... 40
REMOVING RUST FROM CAST IRON.......................... 41
REMOVING WATER STAINS FROM LEATHER ................ 41
REVIVING LEATHER UPHOLSTERY........................... 41
TARNISHED COPPER........................................... 41
TOILET CLEANER ............................................. 41
VINYL FLOOR CLEANING ...................................... 41
WAXING A FLOOR ............................................. 41

## ANTIQUE APPLIANCES

For cleaning antique appliances: Pour white vinegar straight out of the bottle onto a sponge to soak stubborn buildup for a few minutes. After your appliance's first-time cleaning, future quick cleanups are easiest using a small spray/squirt bottle with a diluted vinegar-water mixture.

## BRASSWARE

To clean brassware without scrubbing, soak in 1 part of white vinegar to 10 parts of water. To clean brass lamps, unscrew the sections and soak in bucket. All the green and black tarnish comes off in no time.

## CARPET SPOT AND STAIN REMOVER

As a carpet spot and stain remover, take a trigger spray bottle and fill with one part white vinegar to seven parts water. Saturate the stain with the vinegar solution and let it soak in for a few minutes. Next blot thoroughly with an old towel to remove excess moisture. Repeat until the stain has gone.

## CLEANING A SHOWERHEAD

Clean a showerhead by unscrewing it to remove the rubber washer. Place the head in a pot filled with equal parts vinegar and water, bring to a boil, then simmer for five minutes. Alternatively, soak the showerhead in vinegar overnight, then rinse in hot water to keep it flowing freely.

## CLEANING A WHIRLPOOL TUB

Pour 1 gallon (3.75 liters) of white vinegar into the water of a whirlpool tub, once a year and run it. This will keep the jets from clogging up from soap scum, etc.

## CLEANING DRAINS

Keep your drains clean and working properly with vinegar. When they seem to be getting a bit sluggish, or even blocked, pour white vinegar down the kitchen and bathroom sinks and shower drain.

## CLEANING FIREPLACE DOORS

Put vinegar on newspaper and use to wipe down the insides of glass fireplace doors. Cleans instantly and does not streak.

## CLEANING FLUID FOR COPPER AND BRASS

Make a brass and copper cleaner by combining equal parts of lemon juice and vinegar. Wipe it on a paper towel and then polish with a soft, dry cloth.

## CLEANING METAL SCREENS AND ALUMINUM FURNITURE

Use vinegar to clean away mineral build-up on metal. Add 3 tablespoons to 4 cups (1 liter) of water for cleaning metal screens and aluminum furniture.

## CLEANING PORCELAIN, ENAMEL BATHS AND SINKS

Use a half-and-half solution of vinegar and water.

## FLOOR CLEANER

Add ⅔ cup (150 ml) vinegar to 1 gallon (3.75 liters) of water to keep your vinyl floors clean and shining.

## FURNITURE POLISH

Make a furniture polish using equal parts of white vinegar and vegetable oil. Wipe it on and buff with a soft cloth.

## HARD WATER DEPOSITS

Use vinegar to get rid of the hard water deposits around your sink. Soak paper towels with vinegar and place them around the area that needs to be cleaned. For cleaning the tap you can soak the towel and wrap it around and then hold it in place with a rubber band. Do this overnight and the next morning it's easy to wipe clean. This is safe for brass taps as well.

## REMOVING LIME DEPOSITS

Use one part vinegar to one part water to clean tiles and grouting. On newer tiles, test in an inconspicuous area first, especially if colored grouting has been used.

## REMOVING RUST FROM CAST IRON

Make a white vinegar solution that is 2 parts vinegar to 1 part water, to clean the rust off cast iron pans. Soak the pan overnight in the vinegar solution and the vinegar just dissolves the rust. Very rusty pans may take an extra evening. Don't leave a pan in there too long, or you will not have a pan! The vinegar dissolves the metal.

## REMOVING WATER STAINS FROM LEATHER

Remove water stains from leather by rubbing with a cloth dipped in a vinegar-and-water solution.

## REVIVING LEATHER UPHOLSTERY

Leather can be revived by wiping with a damp cloth sprinkled with a little white vinegar.

## TARNISHED COPPER

If you have a heavily tarnished copper or copper alloy object to be cleaned up, use a paste made of salt and vinegar.

## TOILET CLEANER

Remove stubborn stains from the toilet by spraying them with vinegar and brushing vigorously. Deodorize the bowl by adding 2½ cups (570 ml) of distilled vinegar. Allow it to remain for half an hour before flushing.

## VINYL FLOOR CLEANING

For effortless cleaning and less bending, try squirting vinegar on the head of a moistened mop and wiping over the floor. Environmentally friendly and cheap!

## WAXING A FLOOR

When waxing a floor after scrubbing with a floor stripper, add 1 cup (225 ml) of vinegar to the rinse water. It neutralizes the chemicals and makes the wax or floor finish adhere better.

## GREEN AIR FRESHENERS AND ODOR CONTROL

AIR FRESHENER ........ 43
AROMATIC VINEGAR AIR FRESHENER ........ 43
CLEANING HUMIDIFIERS ........ 43
HAND CLEANER ........ 43
REMOVING PAINT FUMES ........ 43
REMOVING THE SMELL OF ANIMAL URINE ........ 43
REMOVING THE SMELL OF ONIONS ........ 43
REMOVING THE SMELL OF VOMIT/SOUR MILK ........ 44
RIDDING THE AIR OF STALE SMOKE OR PERFUME ........ 44
SPONGE/CLOTH RESTORER ........ 44
TO REMOVE COOKING ODORS ........ 44

## AIR FRESHENER

Use a teaspoon of baking soda, 1 tablespoon of vinegar and 2½ cups (570 ml) of water. After it stops foaming, mix well and use in a spray bottle.

## AROMATIC VINEGAR AIR FRESHENER

Add approximately 1¾ oz (15 g) each of sage, rosemary, mint, rue, and wormwood to 2½ cups (570 ml) of wine or cider vinegar. Allow the herbs to stand in the vinegar for about a week in a warm place. Strain and use as an air freshener or to control unpleasant smells.

## CLEANING HUMIDIFIERS

Rinse out humidifiers every few days and add two tablespoons of vinegar to prevent mold and bacteria from forming. Running this in the bathroom with the door and window closed will eliminate mold. Rinse and run again with clean water. It's important to renew the water each time instead of just filling up the reservoir.

## HAND CLEANER

Remove cooking smells from hands by rinsing them with vinegar and then wash thoroughly with soap and water.

## REMOVING PAINT FUMES

Absorb the odor of fresh paint by putting a small dish of white vinegar in the room.

## REMOVING THE SMELL OF ANIMAL URINE

Blot up the urine with a soft cloth and wash several times with lukewarm water. Apply a mixture of equal parts vinegar and cool water. Blot up again, rinse, and let dry.

## REMOVING THE SMELL OF ONIONS

A little white vinegar rubbed on your fingers before and after slicing onions will remove the smell of onions quickly.

### REMOVING THE SMELL OF VOMIT/SOUR MILK

To rid the smell after an unfortunate bout of sickness, clean the area thoroughly, then place a bowl of vinegar on the floor and leave overnight. This works very well in a car as well, especially in warm weather. Leave the bowl on the floor of the car overnight, with the doors and windows shut.

### RIDDING THE AIR OF STALE SMOKE OR PERFUME

Keep a vinegar-and-water solution handy in a spray bottle for use after smokers have left. Even if they're not smoking, the smell can still be a problem. This is also good for clearing the air of residual scent after visitors wearing unpleasant aftershave or perfume have left.

### SPONGE/CLOTH RESTORER

If a sponge, washcloth, or dishcloth becomes slimy or smelly, soak overnight in a solution of half vinegar/half water. Rinse in clear water and leave to dry.

### TO REMOVE COOKING ODORS

Boil a teaspoon of white vinegar mixed in 1 cup (225 ml) of water to eliminate unpleasant cooking odors.

## HOME DECORATING AND RENOVATING

BASIC WOOD CLEANING SOLUTION .......... 46
CLEANING RAW WOOD .......... 46
CLEANING VARNISHED WOOD .......... 46
CLEANING WOODEN PANELING .......... 46
FABRIC AND LEATHER GLUE .......... 47
HAND CARE AFTER PLASTER OR CLAY WORK .......... 47
PAINTING .......... 47
PREPARATION FOR PAINTING .......... 47
PREVENT PLASTER FROM DRYING OUT TOO QUICKLY .... 47
REMOVING GLUE FROM OLD FURNITURE .......... 47
REMOVING GRIME FROM FURNITURE .......... 47
REMOVING RING STAINS .......... 48
REMOVING TEMPERA PAINT .......... 48
REVIVING AN OLD STOVE OR FIREPLACE .......... 48
REVIVING OLD LEATHERWORK .......... 48
SOFTEN PAINTBRUSHES .......... 48
WALLPAPER PASTE SOLVENT .......... 48

## BASIC WOOD CLEANING SOLUTION

This is a good mix for well-used furniture. The vinegar does a wonderful job of pulling dirt out of wood.

3 tablespoons white distilled vinegar
3 tablespoons water
½ teaspoon liquid soap or detergent
A few drops of olive oil

Combine the ingredients in a bowl, saturate a sponge with the mixture, and squeeze out the excess to wash surfaces. The smell of vinegar will disappear in a few hours.

Always store carefully in a labeled jar or bottle.

## CLEANING RAW WOOD

White vinegar can also be used to clean raw wood, such as a wooden cutting board. Pour undiluted vinegar onto the wood and then use a sponge to literally push the dirt away. Be sure to wipe in the direction of the wood grain, starting at one end and working to the other. This way the dirt you are trying to get rid of won't be pushed back into the wood grain.

## CLEANING VARNISHED WOOD

If varnished wood has taken on a cloudy appearance but the cloudiness hasn't gone through to the wood, it can be removed by rubbing the wood with a soft cloth soaked in a solution of 1 tablespoon of distilled vinegar in 4 cups (1 liter) of lukewarm water. Wring out the cloth and rub into the wood. Complete the job by wiping the surface with a soft dry cloth.

## CLEANING WOODEN PANELING

Clean wood paneling with a mixture of one part olive oil to two parts of distilled vinegar in 4 cups (1 liter) of warm water. Moisten a soft cloth with the solution and wipe the paneling. The yellowing is then removed by wiping with a soft, dry cloth.

## FABRIC AND LEATHER GLUE

Vinegar makes excellent fabric/leather glue:

1 envelope clear gelatin
3 tablespoons of white vinegar
3–4 tablespoons of water
1 teaspoon of glycerine

Melt the gelatin and water over a low heat, then add the other ingredients and mix well. Apply while warm. Store the remaining glue in a small plastic or glass jar. Warm it up next time before use.

## HAND CARE AFTER PLASTER OR CLAY WORK

This tip came from a professional artist. You can rebalance the pH of the alkali in the material if you wash your hands with soap, then rinse well with a one-to-one solution of white vinegar and water each time.

## PAINTING

Painting adheres better to galvanized metal after it has been brushed with vinegar.

## PREPARATION FOR PAINTING

Wiping down clean metal surfaces with a vinegar solution (1 part vinegar to 5 parts water) prepares the surface for painting and reduces the incidence of peeling.

## PREVENT PLASTER FROM DRYING OUT TOO QUICKLY

Prevent plaster from drying too quickly when patching or filling in by adding one tablespoon of vinegar to the water when mixing. This will slow the drying time.

## REMOVING GLUE FROM OLD FURNITURE

To loosen old glue around rungs and joints of tables and chairs being repaired, apply distilled vinegar with a small oil can.

## REMOVING GRIME FROM FURNITURE

Dirt and grime can be easily removed from woodwork with a solution of 1 cup (225 ml) of ammonia, ⅔ cup

(150 ml) of distilled vinegar, and 2½ tablespoons (30 g) of baking soda dissolved in warm water. This solution will not dull the finish or leave streaks. Be careful of the smell when you mix these together.

### REMOVING RING STAINS

Stubborn rings left where wet glasses have been placed on wood furniture can be removed by rubbing them with a mixture of equal parts of distilled vinegar and olive oil. Rub with the grain and polish for the best results.

### REMOVING TEMPERA PAINT

Vinegar works well to remove tempera paint, or the type of paint you use when you decorate your windows for Halloweeen or Christmas. It takes it off almost immediately. Sponge vinegar over the paint, then wipe off, removing residual paint with paper towels.

### REVIVING AN OLD STOVE OR FIREPLACE

All grease spots must be washed off and any rust removed, and the stove must be cold. Mix black lead with vinegar to a creamy consistency and apply to the metal areas of the stove or fireplace. Polish with a stiff brush when nearly dry.

### REVIVING OLD LEATHERWORK

Mix a scant cup (200 ml) of vinegar with 1¾ cup (400 ml) of linseed oil. Shake this in a bottle until it reaches the consistency of cream. Rub into the leather and polish with a soft cloth.

### SOFTEN PAINTBRUSHES

Soak a paintbrush in hot vinegar, then wash out with warm, soapy water to soften it up.

### WALLPAPER PASTE SOLVENT

Vinegar makes a great solvent for wallpaper paste. Just dilute 1 cup (225 ml) of white vinegar with 2 quarts (2-3 liters) of very warm water, and apply generously with a sponge. Once you get an edge or corner of the wallpaper to lift, then start working the vinegar solution behind the paper to break down the adhesive. This process is most effective when you keep your work area very damp—let the warmth of the water and the chemical properties of the vinegar do the work for you.

Rinse your sponge often and mix a new batch of vinegar-and-water solution when it becomes cool and/or murky. The bonus is that vinegar is inexpensive and it will not stain or discolor carpeting or other flooring.

## MISCELLANEOUS GREEN USES

BIODEGRADABLE BUG AND FLY SPRAY ...................... 51
CLEANING DENTURES.......................................... 51
CLEANING PHOTOCOPIER GLASS ............................ 51
CLEANING SILK FLOWER ARRANGEMENTS.................. 51
CLEANING EYEGLASSES ...................................... 51
GETTING RID OF FRUIT FLIES ............................... 51
NEW WICKS ..................................................... 52
NYLON PANTYHOSE ........................................... 52
PERKING UP CUT FLOWERS ................................. 52
PREVENTING FADING OF EMBROIDERY THREAD .......... 52
REMOVING A PERFUME YOU DON'T LIKE ................. 52
REMOVING STICKERS ......................................... 52
SHINY PATENT LEATHER ..................................... 52
SHOE CLEANER ................................................ 53
SMOOTHER NAIL POLISH ..................................... 53
PETS AND ANIMALS ............................................53

**BIODEGRADABLE BUG AND FLY SPRAY**

Spraying bugs inside the home means that you get chemicals on carpets and furniture. Try filling an old water pistol with vinegar. You can then spray the offending insect without damaging the décor. This is alleged to work on cockroaches as well.

**CLEANING DENTURES**

To clean dentures leave them in vinegar for as long as you would leave them in a denture cleanser – about 15 minutes to half an hour. Then brush them thoroughly.

**CLEANING PHOTOCOPIER GLASS**

Keep a solution of one to two tablespoons vinegar and water in a small spray bottle for cleaning glass screens.

**CLEANING SILK FLOWER ARRANGEMENTS**

Use a spray bottle filled with vinegar. When they get dusty, spray them lightly, and the dust is gone. They also look brand new!

**CLEANING EYEGLASSES**

Eyeglasses will clean up and be free of streaks when wiped down with water to which a splash of vinegar has been added. (Note: Rum works well too!)

**GETTING RID OF FRUIT FLIES**

Put a bowl of cider vinegar out to attract fruit flies. The same can be achieved by washing the windows with cider vinegar, but that's probably not the effect you want.
If this just attracts the flies but doesn't kill them, put one teaspoon of sugar, two teaspoons of cider vinegar, and several drops of dish-washing liquid in a small shallow plastic container. Fill up with water. The flies will be attracted to the vinegar, but the soap will kill them.

Alternatively, take a small bowl and partially fill it with vinegar, then wrap it in plastic wrap. Poke a few pinholes in the plastic wrap, and the fruit flies will fly in but can't get out. Place the bowl wherever you see the fruit flies.

### NEW WICKS

Soak new propane lantern wicks in vinegar for several hours. Let them dry before using. The wicks will burn longer and brighter.

### NYLON PANTYHOSE

When washing your pantyhose, add vinegar to the water to prolong their lifespan.

### PERKING UP CUT FLOWERS

Keep cut flowers fresh longer by adding two tablespoons of vinegar and one tablespoon of sugar to each 4 cups (1 liter) of water.

### PREVENTING FADING OF EMBROIDERY THREAD

Dip the whole skein of thread in white vinegar and then let dry. This sets the dye, so when washing an embroidered item there will be no running of colors.

### REMOVING A PERFUME YOU DON'T LIKE

It is generally recommended in the trade that vinegar removes the smell of a perfume you don't like. Just apply it to the skin that has been sprayed with the undesired perfume.

### REMOVING STICKERS

Remove stickers by soaking a cloth in vinegar and covering for several minutes until the vinegar soaks in. The stickers should then peel off easily.

### SHINY PATENT LEATHER

Patent leather will shine better if you wipe it with a soft cloth that has been moistened with distilled vinegar.

### SHOE CLEANER

Remove winter salt stains from shoes by wiping with a cloth dampened in a vinegar solution. Use 1 tablespoon vinegar to 1 cup (225 ml) of water.

## SMOOTHER NAIL POLISH

Nail polish will go on smoother and stay on longer if you clean your fingernails with white vinegar before applying the polish.

## PETS AND ANIMALS

### Removing and preventing fleas

Adding cider vinegar to drinking water discourages fleas from setting up home on dogs and cats. Start with just a few drops so that your pets get used to the taste, then build up a little, to a teaspoon per bowl for a small animal, to a tablespoon for a larger pet.

Alternatively, dip your pet in a bath of cider vinegar and water. This is, apparently, suitable treatment for puppies that are too young for commercial chemical treatments. Avoid getting any vinegar in your pet's eyes.

### Removing a tear duct stain from white-haired dogs

Tear stains are caused by the acidity in a dog's system. By putting a few drops of vinegar into the animal's drinking water, you will help to neutralize the acidity. Within a few weeks the tear stains should disappear.

### Vinegar for rabbit breeding

If your doe is unreceptive for breeding, try adding one tablespoon of white vinegar to her fresh water. After 24 hours the doe will be very receptive, and the buck will be happy too!

### Vinegar for chickens

Add vinegar to chickens' water, especially in the winter, to keep them laying better and staying healthy. Apparently, it also helps to deter the chickens from pecking each other.

### For reducing swelling

For reducing the swelling on a horse's leg (or any other animal for that matter), wrap the leg in a rag soaked in cider vinegar. Wrap in plastic and then bandage to hold it in place. Leave on for four hours or more.

### For cleaning fish tanks

Use white vinegar to clean the mineral deposits that accumulate at the top of your fish tank. Soak some paper towels in the vinegar and simply wipe around the inside of the tank where the water has evaporated and left the white mineral deposits. You can also use vinegar to clean aquarium ornaments. It is harmless to fish so you don't need to worry if some of the vinegar happens to get into the water.

### Keeping flies away from horses

Mix ⅓ vinegar (any type, but cider vinegar smells better), ⅓ water and ⅓ bath oil in a spray bottle. This makes a good fly spray for horses and other animals – dogs and goats for example – as well as a barn spray for keeping flies down.

# BAKING SODA

# INTRODUCTION

## WHAT IS BAKING SODA?

Baking soda, a white chemical compound, has also been known as:

- sodium bicarbonate
- saleratus
- bicarbonate of soda
- bread soda
- sodium hydrogen carbonate

For the more scientifically minded, the chemical formula is:

$$NaHCO_3$$

| Sodium bicarbonate |
|---|
| $Na^+ - O \diagdown C \diagup OH$, with $C = O$ (double bond to O below C) |

These symbols show you the constituent parts of this chemical compound. Sodium bicarbonate is made from the elements carbon (C), hydrogen (H), oxygen (O), and sodium (Na). It can be reproduced by the Solvay process, which involves the reaction of sodium chloride, ammonia, and carbon dioxide and produces over 100,000 tons per year. Commercial quantities of baking soda are also produced when soda ash, mined in the form of the ore trona, is dissolved in water and treated with carbon dioxide.

As a solid it is not totally soluble in water. It is crystalline in appearance but often looks like a powder. The Na in the chemical formula comes from natron, a substance known to be used as far back as ancient Egyptian times, and found in many mineral springs. It has a taste resembling that of sodium carbonate and is alkaline in terms of pH value (8.3). Baking soda is considered to be relatively safe to use, without harming the skin, but ingesting large amounts should be avoided.

Sodium is a soft, silver-white metallic element, one of the alkali metals, found in soda, salt, and other compounds.

To avoid confusion, the following are not the same as baking soda, although they have similar names and some similar constituents:

- Baking powder, which contains baking soda
- Sodium chloride, or common salt
- Sodium hydroxide or caustic soda
- Sodium carbonate, known as soda ash, sodium decahydrate, and washing soda

These all have wide-ranging applications and effects. You can find out more about all of these sodium-related substances in the glossary.

**SODIUM**

Knowing a little about the properties of sodium helped me to understand why baking soda is such a useful substance for domestic purposes. I even began to wish I could go back and learn a bit more chemistry. As a 14 year old I wasn't remotely interested or motivated, probably because of the chalk and talk approach, rather than creating chemical changes and observing reactions.

Sodium exists as more than a trace element in the stars and the sun and is the sixth most abundant element on the earth's crust, making up an estimated 2.8 percent. Sodium, along with potassium, is classed as a soft metal but is not found naturally as a metal. It is found in a wide distribution as compounds with other substances, the most familiar being sodium chloride or table salt. Other salts of sodium are found in many rocks and in nearly all soil types. These include halides, silicates, carbonates, sulfates, and nitrates. Sodium occurs throughout the rocky crust of the earth as feldspar, a silicate of sodium, and in various other rocks. Along with potassium, sodium is a soft metal with a silvery white luster. It tarnishes in the air and is among the most reactive of metals.

Early civilizations knew about the benefits of sodium, although because potassium compounds were very similar in appearance, they thought they were the same substance. Records exist of saltpeter from potassium being used to make glazes for pots in Mesopotamia in the 17th century BC and the Egyptians used sodium carbonate in the 16th century BC for making glass. They also used natron for embalming and preserving.

From early times sodium carbonate was prepared by passing water through the ashes of plants that had been burned. The water was then evaporated from the solution. Soda as a term was first used for either sodium or potassium but later was used to refer to ash produced from sea plants. Potash was used for ash produced from land vegetation. The name potash, incidentally, originated from the use of large pots for evaporating the water from the solution.

Over the years soda and potash were defined as both natural and artificial products and as vegetable and mineral. Imagine playing the old favorite "20 Questions" with the ancestors—it was hard enough trying to define substances as animal, vegetable, or mineral as a science game with elementary school children, but at least they have a better understanding of materials in today's schools. Another nugget of information that might corner your imagination for a split second: It wasn't until the beginning of the 19th century that Sir Humphry Davy decomposed both alkalis and called them sodium and potassium, which are really Latinized versions of soda and potash. The two metals cannot be isolated by normal chemical processes and were only prepared after the discovery of the electric current in 1800, when the electrolytic processes were developed. Davy's method was modified and called the Castner process and was used to prepare sodium for a long time. Most is now prepared by the Down's process, which produces chlorine as well as sodium.

Sodium chemicals today are used widely in synthetic chemistry as drying agents and reducing agents. Sodium has also been used in the manufacture of photoelectric cells. Its high heat capacity and conductivity make it useful as a heat transfer medium. It is lighter than water and can be cut with a knife at room temperature. It reacts with water to give hydrogen and sodium hydroxide, so it is an extremely active chemical that easily unites with oxygen. The metal is, therefore, usually kept immersed in an inert liquid for safety. It is used in some nuclear reactors, and sodium lights give that characteristic yellow illumination to many of our roads and towns. This works by gaseous sodium glowing in a tube that has voltage passed through it.

## GREEN APPLICATIONS OF BAKING SODA

Baking soda has many uses in a number of areas, but the most well-known domestic uses are related to cooking and household cleaning jobs. There are many other commercial applications, however, including use in some fire extinguishers, as a deodorizer, and as a neutralizer of acids.

### GOING UP . . .

Baking soda is used in cooking as a raising agent. Bakery products are aerated by gas bubbles, either developed naturally or by being folded in from the atmosphere. The natural method of leavening bread is achieved by the addition of yeast, by bacterial fermentation, or from chemical reaction, such as that produced by the addition of baking soda. All bread produced commercially—except rye bread and salt-rising/soda bread varieties—uses yeast to make it rise. Cakes, cookies, and other bakery products are leavened by carbon dioxide, which is produced when baking soda is added. On its own, however, baking soda makes dough alkaline and causes deterioration in flavor and discoloration, so an acid reaction substance is also added to the baking soda to make it into baking powder.

### ANYONE FOR LEMONADE?

Before the advent of readily available carbonated drinks, our Victorian ancestors knew how to use baking soda to make a bubbly lemonade, although you had to drink it quickly, before all the bubbles escaped. What used to be known as “pop” (thanks to the gassy bubbles) was certainly what children knew and loved as soda pop, originally served up through a soda fountain. Today, in France, if you order a carbonated soft drink in a café, the itemized check may well list it simply as “soda”.

### OUT, FOUL SPOT!

Baking soda has long been used for a variety of cleaning

purposes in the bathroom and kitchen. It can be used to deodorize the refrigerator, diapers, and garbage cans, and to clean out drains and remove soap scum. Many other uses are described later in the book.

### PAIN RELIEF

Baking soda has been used as a remedy for acid indigestion and heartburn. It makes blood and urine less acidic and increases the sodium in the body, but it should not be used long term without consulting a doctor. It also relieves bee stings, nettle rash, and sunburn.

### SPLAT THAT GNAT!

As a deterrent to ants and fleas, baking soda is a cheap, fairly harmless alternative to commercial products. Smelly pets can be made sweeter smelling when cleaned with baking soda.

### WHITE TEETH AND LUSTROUS LOCKS

Used in toothpaste, baking soda helps to remove stains and freshen breath. When used during hair washing, it can help remove buildup of other products and give your hair an extra shine.

### STOP THAT FIRE!

Baking soda has long been used in dry chemical fire extinguishers to put out electrical or flammable liquid fires. Baking soda works by interrupting the flame is chain reaction. This chemical agent is one of the main chemicals used as a powder in the mixtures of dry chemicals stored in pressurized tanks or containers. These can be put onto vehicles or into portable extinguishers in advance and are pressurized by an inert gas, such as carbon dioxide, nitrogen, helium, or argon. When discharged, they replace the oxygen in the air that would otherwise feed the fire. Carbon dioxide is the most commonly used propellant and the action starts by puncturing the seal of a cartridge of the liquefied gas. Before this method became common, soda-acid fire extinguishers generated carbon dioxide by mixing a solution of baking soda with sulfuric acid. So there we have two applications of sodium bicarbonate in dealing with fires. Portable dry chemical fire extinguishers are designed to reach 6 to 15 ft (2 to 5 m) and discharge in about 10 to 15 seconds, so the chemical reaction achieved is both impressive and effective.

## NEUTRALIZING ACID SPILLS

Baking soda is commonly used for neutralizing acid spills, such as battery acid.

Another surprising fact to the uninitiated, like me, is that it is used to counteract the effects of white phosphorus in incendiary bullets spreading in wounds to the body.

## QUICK SOLUTION

Equally common is the use of baking soda to increase the pH and alkalinity of water in a swimming pool or spa. It is added as a solution for restoring the balance of water where a high chlorine level exists. It can also be added to septic tanks to control pH and maintain the correct conditions for bacterial activity.

# GLOSSARY

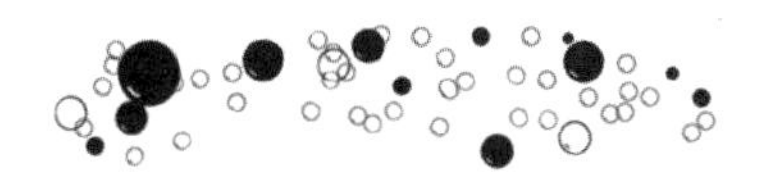

Because there are so many similar sounding names and applications for sodium compounds, I thought it might be useful to describe them all in lay terms—in other words, in terms that I understand!

**BAKING POWDER**

This is a mixture of baking soda and one or more acid salts, such as tartaric acid (cream of tartar) or sodium aluminum sulfate, which creates a chemical reaction where carbon dioxide is released. A drying agent, such as cornstarch, is also added. The precise mix determines whether the baking powder is a single- or double-acting powder. Baking powder has a fairly short shelf life of 6–12 months, unlike baking soda, which keeps for longer.

Single-acting baking powder produces a chemical reaction in the bowl when the baking soda comes into contact with a liquid. Double-acting baking powder starts the reaction in the bowl but reacts again when the mixture is heated.

**BAKING SODA**

This is also known as sodium bicarbonate, sodium hydrogen carbonate, bicarbonate of soda, saleratus, and bread soda. It is a white, crystalline powder or granular salt that is soluble in water. It is used in the manufacture of carbonated drinks and baking powder and is also a component of fire extinguishers. Medical uses include counteracting stomach and urinary acidity, cleaning mucous membranes, and dressing burns.

When used for cooking, baking soda must be used with an acid to start a reaction. This may be provided by, amongst other ingredients, sugar, honey, yogurt, citrus juice, or fruit.

## CREAM OF TARTAR

This is the most commonly known and widely used leavening acid that is contained in baking powder.
If you use baking soda as a leavener, the mix needs to include an acid, such as that found in sugar, yogurt, fruit, or cocoa. Cream of tartar provides the acid needed to cause a reaction with moisture in the mix, usually milk or water.

Cream of tartar is a white sediment found lining the inside of wine caskets after fermentation (tartaric acid). This sediment can be removed and used to produce a fine white powder.

## PEARLASH

Potash is the ashes from roots and treestumps that have been strained again and again with hot water and then boiled down until a residue of brown ash was left. When potash was put into an oven and continuously stirred, it would eventually become "pearlash." Pearlash was worth far more than potash, and by the mid-1700s pearlash production had evolved into a major industry and exports of ash from the American colonies were established in Britain for use in the glass industry and soap factories. During the 1760s, pearlash became a popular substitute for yeast in baking.

## SALERATUS

The name comes from the Latin *sal aeratus,* which means aerated salt, and it was used by doctors as a safe treatment for acid indigestion. In Europe, chemists put carbon dioxide gas through solutions of sodium carbonate to form less alkaline sodium bicarbonate. This became known as saleratus. Bakers in North America discovered that European baking soda was superior to the pearlash they had been using. This product was more reliable and gave less of a bitter aftertaste.

**SODIUM CARBONATE (SODA ASH, SODIUM DECAHYDRATE, OR WASHING SODA)**

Sodium carbonate is a constituent of many mineral waters and occurs as the main salt component in sodium bicarbonate. It is used as a general cleaner and has many industrial applications. In medicine, it is used to treat skin inflammation and to clean parts of the body. Sold as washing soda, it is a cheap but effective household cleaning agent and useful for washing heavily soiled fabric. It is efficient at unblocking grease from drains and for cleaning sinks. It has been used in the photographic process and in brick making. Sodium carbonate should not be confused with baking soda for cooking, because it has a pH of 11 and is, therefore, not suitable for consumption.

**SODIUM CHLORIDE (COMMON SALT)**

This is the most abundant form of sodium. It is the main salt in seawater, making up 80 percent of the dissolved matter. There are extensive worldwide deposits which probably originated from the evaporation of prehistoric seas. Sodium chloride is present in all body fluids and is essential to human and animal life. Common salt is also used for preserving food and seasoning, as well as in the manufacture of dyes, soaps, ceramic glazes, leather curing, and the production of many chemicals.

**SODIUM FLUORIDE**

This is a mix of sodium carbonate and hydrofluoric acid. It is used as an insecticide and pesticide and is fatal if ingested. Curiously though, when added in minute quantities to municipal drinking water, it reduces dental decay.

## SODIUM HYDROXIDE (CAUSTIC SODA, ALSO KNOWN AS LYE)

This is a white, moisture-attracting solid, obtained by electrolysis from a solution of sodium chloride. It is highly corrosive to plants and animals. When dissolved in water it forms an alkaline solution, which neutralizes acids in many commercial processes, including refining petroleum, soap, and detergent manufacture and making paper, cellophane, and rayon.

## SODIUM NITRATE

This occurs naturally as Chile saltpeter and can be manufactured from sodium carbonate and nitric acid. It is used to make fertilizers, glass, pottery enamels, matches, explosives, and dyes. Worryingly, to a novice like me, it is also used in preserving meat.

## SODIUM PEROXIDE

This is an oxidizing agent for bleaching paper, cloth, wood, ivory, and for purifying the air in confined spaces such as submarines or airplanes.

## SODIUM SULPHATE (GLAUBER'S SALTS)

This was discovered by Johann Glauber in the 17th century as a natural mineral in the form of mirabilite. A neutral salt, it is used for detergents, glass, and paper making and in dyeing and printing textiles. It was originally used as a laxative.

# USES OF BAKING SODA THROUGHOUT HISTORY

## NATRON

**DROP-DEAD GORGEOUS**

The ancient Egyptians appreciated beauty so much they protected and preserved it even after death by mummification. A major substance in this process was natron, a white crystalline mixture of sodium bicarbonate, sodium carbonate, sodium chloride, and sodium sulfate. It was mined from dry lake beds and from the banks of the River Nile. The area of Wadi-el-Natrun lies 75 ft (23 m) below sea level and gets its name from the natron. Known to be mildly antiseptic as well as a good exfoliant and drying substance, it was, all in all, a perfect base for adding oils and fragrances used to preserve the dead. The fragrances exemplified spirituality and beauty and served to cover up the foul odors of decaying flesh, which conjured up or summoned particular deities. So you not only had to look good but also smell divine, even in the intense heat of Egypt, without refrigeration or air-conditioning.

**HOLISTIC CLEANER**

The ancient Egyptians recognized that cleanliness was of the utmost importance in the living as well as the dead. Natron was the supreme, holistic, cleaning product and was used in a variety of ways for personal hygiene and household cleaning. To ensure you were really clean and pure, you needed to smell clean and not give off bad odors that might summon up evil forces. The closest you can get today to natron is a box of commercially produced baking soda. Many of the age-old remedies and applications of baking soda can be traced back, like so many other seemingly modern remedies, to the knowledge possessed by the ancient Egyptians.

### MUMMY'S MULTIPURPOSE MATE

As well as for mummification, the Egyptians were known to have used natron for:

- Ridding the home of vermin
- Cleaning the body as an exfoliant
- Cleaning teeth
- Preventing body odor
- Cleaning cuts
- Making a light to paint tombs by
- Making glass

As an ancient toothpaste, natron could be mixed with a few drops of water to create a paste. A few drops of myrrh, the resin derived from thorny desert trees in modern Ethiopia, Yemen, and Somalia, could also be added. Myrrh was much prized by the Egyptians as a perfume, incense, and healer, and they believed that, when it was added to the toothpaste, it served as a gum protector and improver of oral hygiene.

Added to castor oil, natron provided a smokeless fuel by which painters and artisans could work in the ancient tombs without creating harmful smoke and soot, which might spoil the work.

## NATRON AND GLASS-MAKING

Pliny the Elder claimed that the invention of glass took place on the Palestinian coast, when natron merchant ships were sailing from Egypt to the mouth of the River Belus near Ptolemais. The crews needed stones to hold up their cooking pots but, because these were in short supply, they used some of the natron as a substitute. The heat from the fire caused the natron, rich in sodium, to fuse with the surrounding sand, when the fire became too intense, and produced a new material—glass. This story has been challenged over the years, however, because the temperature of the fire would not have been great enough to cause fusion.

Another theory suggests that glass invention occurred around 2200 BC in Iran. Coloration of glass was already understood by the time Tutankhamun reigned, around 1330 BC. Colored glass was used in furniture and architecture from then onward, but it was the Romans who really played a major role in industrializing the process around the Mediterranean region.

**ROMAN GLASS**

The Romans made glass from two types of materials, one of which included natron, which came from Egypt. When spring came, the lakes evaporated, exposing the deposits of natron around the edges and in the lake beds. The Romans used this to produce glass on a large scale from about 500 BC to AD 850. Before this time, glass was considered as a product for decorative use rather than for its many more practical uses. It was manufactured by melting alkali (potash or sodium) with silica, such as quartz or sand. Different semiprecious stones provided different colors—for example turquoise, created a pale blue glass, and fluorite, a purple hue.

**WORLD GLASS**

During the next several hundred years, glass developed in different ways in various parts of the world, and was based on either soda or potash. The soda was found in Mediterranean regions in the ashes of plants in sea marshes and in seaweed. Germany and Bohemia used potash from beech wood, and France used bracken as a source. The quality of the glass depended on the preparation of the soda.

Lead glass or flint glass was invented in the 17th century, in the days of William and Mary of Orange, in the Netherlands. This could be cut to enhance designs and show off its sheen. After this, there were still more changes and refinements to glass and its production; for example, large amounts of lead were used with potash and Venetian glass was produced with soda. Flint glass was made from three parts sand, two parts red lead and one part potash or pearl ash from Canada or Russia.

### BLOWN AWAY

Europe seemed to have the monopoly on expensive and decorative blown glassware until a carpenter in Massachusetts, invented a new method of pressed glass in 1827. Then, in 1864 in Western Virginia, William Leighton brought about a revolution in the process of making glass at a fraction of the price of the lead and flint varieties. His pressed glass was of equally good clarity and could be produced thinly by being pressed into a mold. The major difference though, was the use of baking soda and lime instead of lead. All this and manufactured at one-third of the price! The baking soda was also readily available in large quantities.

### RADIOACTIVE

You may be interested to learn that one particular type of glass made in the United States in the 1880s—known as Burmese glass—contained, alongside baking soda, some rather unusual ingredients, one of which was uranium! This was commonly used to color yellow and green glass for more than a hundred years. Understandably, it was banned during the 1940s, due to health concerns for the glassworkers and also, rather obviously, because of its use in making the atomic bomb. The British Government apparently confiscated huge quantities of materials containing uranium at the end of World War II from glass producers. Quantities of baking soda were also seized.

How about this as a shopping list or recipe for making glass:

- 100 lb white sand
- 36 lb lead oxide
- 25 lb potash
- 7 lb potassium nitrate
- 5 lb baking soda
- 6 lb fluorspar
- 5 lb feldspar

- 2 lb uranium oxide
- 1.5 pennyweights colloidal gold

. . . on reflection, perhaps not!

**THE FAIREST METHOD OF ALL?**
Using baking soda for commercial production of glass has several benefits. It is effective at high temperatures of around 750°F (400°C) and higher. During manufacture the glass gives off acid fumes and dust. Baking soda neutralizes acid components of gases so that they can be discharged into the atmosphere. The residual chemicals of sodium sulphate are recycled in the furnace, using baking soda.

## PEARLASH

As mentioned earlier, baking soda, or baking soda, was first used by American colonists in the form of a refined type of potash called pearlash. By the mid-1700s, production had evolved into a major industry and imports of ash from the colonies, with their abundant supplies of trees to burn, were established in Britain for use in the glass industry and soap factories.

Pearlash was made from potash by baking it in a kiln to remove impurities. This produced a fine white powder. During the 1760s, pearlash became a popular substitute for yeast in baking—yeast took a long time to knead and was, therefore, hard work to do on a regular basis. Since pearlash was alkaline, it was added to the mix to counteract the sourness of sourdough breads, which were leavened from a form of yeast. As well as sweetening the dough, it speeded up the rising time by releasing carbon dioxide bubbles when heated. Pearlash created in minutes what yeast took hours to achieve. This discovery brought about big changes in the baking industry and in the home.

## SALERATUS

The use of baking soda for cooking began in the 18th century. In Europe, chemists put carbon dioxide gas through solutions of sodium carbonate to form less alkaline sodium bicarbonate. This became known as saleratus. The name came from the Latin *sal aeratus,* which means aerated salt, and saleratus was used by doctors as a safe treatment for acid indigestion. Bakers in North America discovered that European baking soda was superior to the pearlash they had been using as a substitute for yeast. This product was expensive but more reliable and gave less of a bitter aftertaste than pearlash.

In the United States saleratus was first made in 1788 when Nathan Read of Massachusetts suspended lumps of pearlash over carbon dioxide fumes produced from fermenting molasses. By the beginning of the 19th century, brewers had started producing saleratus as a by-product, using the carbon dioxide released during fermentation. Because the imports from Europe were expensive, the challenge was to provide an everyday, cheap product in the country. There was also the problem of a slightly hit and miss approach, because the bubbles were often released before the dough made it to the oven. Someone needed to invent a more stable way of adding baking soda for baking.

## DEVELOPMENTS IN LEAVENING AND BAKING

### BAKING POWDER

The first baking powder compounds were created with cream of tartar and baking soda. The mixture gave more consistent results than plain old baking soda, but didn't keep as long and was more costly to use. Experiments continued with calcium phosphate, which still released most of the gas before the cooking stage. Later, sodium aluminum sulfate was discovered and, since it only reacted with the baking soda when heated, baking soda, cornstarch, and the new sulfate were used much more effectively.

In 1843, a British chemist called Alfred Bird made another version of baking powder for his wife Elizabeth, who couldn't eat yeast or eggs. This was so successful that he received an order to supply his fermenting powder to the army. This meant that soldiers could have fresh bread, and the sick and wounded could eat bread, light cakes, light puddings, and other articles of food suited to their condition. He then founded Bird and Son Ltd., who, presumably, went on to make a well-known British custard powder.

Later refinements resulted in the production of single- and double-acting powders. These meant that there was a lot more control over using baking powder in cooking. You can learn more about these in the chemistry and baking sections.

# MINERAL AND CARBONATED DRINKS

**HUBBLE, BUBBLE . . .**

By the 17th century, people were attempting to make refreshing drinks and artificial mineral waters. At first these were required to enhance the experience of medicinal bathing in spas and springs. You could only drink mineral waters if you lived close enough to travel to the source, so there was an opportunity for clever entrepreneurs to invent a substitute and corner potentially huge markets. By the 18th century, companies were producing artificial mineral water in France, Germany, Britain, and Switzerland. In 1788, the "Geneva apparatus" was used for the first industrial production of artificial mineral water. This was achieved by obtaining carbon dioxide from a chemical reaction between sulfur and baking soda, which was then added to a mixing vessel with added salts. But the carbonization did not take place under pressurized conditions, so only a small amount of gas stayed in the water.

In Britain, around 1770, a chemist called Priestly also discovered how carbon dioxide could be added to water. He lived near a brewery, which led him to an understanding of the nature of effervescence found in mineral water. Carbonated drinks today owe much to his early experiments. By 1821, a German doctor and pharmacist in Dresden called Struve had succeeded in inventing a much more sophisticated method of producing artificial mineral water, which resembled the makeup of waters from the Niederselters springs. These became known as seltzers, and soon afterward the production of cheaper soda water was established. If this rings bells, it may be because Alka-Seltzer, a popular remedy for headaches, indigestion, and hangovers in the 20th century, was made from aspirin, baking soda, and citric acid. The "Alka" came from alkaline.

**LEMONADE**

The lemonade much loved by millions today, started life as a flat mineral water flavored with lemons and sweetened with sugar, not so different than it is today. However, mass production of carbonated drinks started during the mid-19th century and the term "lemonade" was used to describe all fruit and berry drinks. The Victorians were very fond of homemade lemonade, as described by Mrs. Beeton and others. The following is based on a 19th-century American recipe for lemonade:

**To make Lemonade:** *Boil two pounds of white sugar with one pint of lemon juice. Bottle and cork. When required, put one tablespoon of the syrup into a tumbler three-quarters full of water. Add one-third teaspoon of baking soda and drink quickly.*

The Victorians also made up powders, which could be conveniently carried on a picnic or when traveling, and reconstituted in a glass of water as required:

***GINGER BEER***

*Put into blue papers 30 grains of baking soda and 5 grains of powdered ginger with a drachm of powdered sugar. Put into white papers, 25 grains of cream of tartar. Put one paper of each kind to half a pint of water.*

(A drachm corresponds roughly to one teaspoon, and 30 grains to half a teaspoon, so 5 grains would be about one-twelfth of a teaspoon.)

# SOAP

## EARLY BATH?

The most common early soaps were made from potash and pearlash. Early references to the use of soap include the Babylonians, about 2800 BC, and the Phoenicians, c.600 BC. The Egyptians used natron, as described above, and the Spaniards and other Mediterranean people were using burned seaweed to provide the alkali they needed. Early uses included the cleaning of wool and cotton fiber prior to spinning and weaving.

## LEND ME YOUR SOAP!

Pliny described Roman soap as being made from goat fat and wood ash, with salt being added to harden it into bars. Excavations in Pompeii have revealed a soap factory with bars of soap. This would have been for textiles rather than personal hygiene, as the Romans favored olive oil and sand to clean their bodies after a good steam.

## THE VERY FIRST SOAP?

Soap is basically a reaction between fatty acids and an alkali. When fats or oils are mixed with a strong alkali the fats are split into fatty acids and glycerine. The sodium or potassium in the alkali joins with the fatty acid as the basis of soap.

The three main stages of early soap making were:

- making a wood ash solution called lye
- cleaning the fats
- boiling the fats with the lye to make soap

Early manufacturers obtained the lye from putting potash into a bottomless barrel over a stone slab, resting on rocks. Straw or sticks were put in the bottom as a sort of strainer and underneath that was placed a collecting container. By slowly pouring water over the ashes, you could produce the lye, a brown liquid dripping down into a container below. This could then be used with the rendered down fat to produce soap. When wood supplies dwindled toward the end of the 18th century, pearlash manufacturing started to decline, making way for more commercial methods. The Leblanc process, described below, changed soap making for ever. Sodium alkalis made harder, better soap without the necessity to add salt.

## COMMERCIAL PRODUCTION OF BAKING SODA

### THE LEBLANC PROCESS

As greater supplies of soda were required for glass-making and soap manufacturing, as well as baking needs, the supplies of ash declined. By the 1700s, production was uneconomical and Europe was being deforested. Potash had to be imported from North America, Russia, and Scandinavia, and Louis XVI in France offered a prize for a method of producing alkali from sea salt. In 1791, Leblanc found a solution, and by 1800 soda ash was being produced at the rate of 10,000 to 15,000 tons per year.

### HOW BROWN WAS MY VALLEY?

After a repeal of a tax on salt in Britain in 1824, the development was unstoppable, and by 1870 the output from Britain had reached 200,000 tons a year—more than all other countries put together. The price was environmental devastation. Sulfuric acid released hydrochloric acid gas into the atmosphere. For every eight tons of soda ash produced, seven tons of calcium sulfide waste hung around on the ground, smelling of rotten eggs. The surrounding land was scorched and fields and gardens produced little that was not spoiled. The people who worked in these factories or who lived close by must have suffered greatly. Luckily, another process was invented without such major disadvantages.

### THE SOLVAY PROCESS

Belgian Ernest Solvay invented a process whereby the only waste product generated was calcium chloride. By 1900, 90 percent of world production used this method. Solvay chemical plants produced about three-quarters of the worldwide requirements, which in 2005 were estimated at 41.9 billion kilograms.

### TRONA DEPOSITS

However, in 1938 in Wyoming, large natural deposits of a mineral called trona were discovered—and sodium carbonate can be extracted more cheaply from trona than by the Solvay method. The name is, as you may have noticed, almost an anagram of natron. I think we've come full circle!

# Green Cleaning Solutions with Baking Soda

# GREEN CLEANING SOLUTIONS WITH BAKING SODA

Baking soda is a cheap, natural cleaning product. It won't break the bank to buy, but it will do the job. Even more importantly, it won't cause harm to the environment in the same way that a number of expensive, caustic products do. Being a natural sceptic, I didn't believe how effective some of the following suggestions could be until I tried them. I'm all in favor of using as few chemicals as possible, as a matter of principle, and the extra effort involved in preparing the pastes and solutions was minimal. As you might also have guessed, housework is not top of my agenda and for some of the kitchen and bathroom jobs I need the incentive of quick, efficient methods! baking soda helps to dissolve grease and dirt and also prevents smells from hanging around.

If you want to make up a solution as an all-purpose cleaner, take two teaspoonfuls of baking soda to 2½ cups (570 ml) of warm water. Adding ½ cup (125 ml) of white vinegar will make an even better cleaner, but beware of the gaseous effect of adding baking soda to vinegar and allow room for expansion. After the fizz has died down, you can pour the mixture into a screw-topped bottle, ready for use.

*CAUTION*

As with all products and cleaning solutions, you should firs try out the suggested method on a small area. I make the following suggestions in good faith and I can't be held responsible for any adverse effects.

First and foremost, don't use baking soda on nonstick pans, or you're likely to ruin the surface.

NOTE: In the following, whenever vinegar is mentioned, please use white vinegar unless told otherwise.

## GREEN KITCHEN USES


BABY BOTTLES .......... 82
BLOCKED DRAINS .......... 82
CLEANING OUT A FOOD PROCESSOR
WITH DRIED-ON FOOD .......... 82
CLEANING THE GARBAGE CAN .......... 82
CLEANING THE BREAD CROCK OR BREAD BOX .......... 82
CLEANING THE DRAIN .......... 83
CLEANING THE EXTERIOR OF WHITE GOODS .......... 83
CLEANING THE REFRIGERATOR .......... 83
CLEANING THE OVEN INTERIOR .......... 84
CLEANING THE TOP OF THE STOVE .......... 84
COFFEEMAKERS .......... 84
DISHWASHERS .......... 84
DISHWASHER POWDER .......... 85
FREEZERS .......... 85
GAS BURNERS .......... 85
GLASS AND STAINLESS STEEL COFFEEPOTS .......... 85
MICROWAVES .......... 85
POTS AND PANS WITH BAKED-ON DEPOSITS .......... 86
REFRESHING A VACUUM FLASK .......... 86
REMOVING GREASE SPILLS .......... 86
REMOVING HARD WATER STAINS .......... 87
REMOVING NEWSPRINT STAINS FROM SURFACES .......... 87
REMOVING PLASTIC WRAPPERS FROM HOT SURFACES .......... 87
REMOVING STAINS FROM COFFEE MUGS .......... 87
REMOVING STAINS ON ENAMELED CAST-IRON WARE .......... 87
STAINLESS STEEL AND CHROME KITCHEN APPLIANCES .......... 88
STAINLESS STEEL SINKS .......... 88
STEEL WOOL PAN SCRUBBERS .......... 88
STUBBORN STAINS ON COUNTERTOPS .......... 88
WASTE DISPOSAL UNITS .......... 89
COUNTERTOPS .......... 90

## BABY BOTTLES

These can be cleaned with a solution of baking soda and water. Be sure to rinse thoroughly.

## BLOCKED DRAIN?

If the tip on page 27 hasn't worked, or you haven't bothered to check for a while, use half a box of baking soda with a cup of warm vinegar. Let this work for an hour or two, then pour down a lot of very hot water. An alternative is to use equal measures of baking soda and table salt, washed down with boiling water.

## CLEANING OUT A FOOD PROCESSOR WITH DRIED-ON FOOD

Of course, this will never happen to you, but some of us are natural slobs. There are always times when the bowl is left in the sink, without soaking, and the blade is stuck away behind a mountain of pots too big for the dishwasher. If you haven't used your blender for a while, it might need just freshening up. Use a couple of teaspoons of baking soda with a cup of warm water, put the lid on and run it for a few seconds. Afterward you can wash as normal, or simply rinse and dry.

## CLEANING THE GARBAGE CAN

Use a fairly strong solution of baking soda and warm water to wash the kitchen garbage can out. It will keep the smell down as well. This is good for all plastic and stainless steel cans.

## CLEANING THE BREAD CROCK OR BREAD BOX

We have a splendid, French deep bread crock that weighs a ton but keeps bread fresh, as long as the odd piece of organic bread isn't left lurking in the bottom out of sight. In this case, the green mold is very smelly, especially if left for a few days in a nice warm kitchen. Washing out with a solution of baking soda in warm water keeps it mold free and sweet smelling. Let dry thoroughly and cool down before storing bread again.

**CLEANING THE DRAIN**

If your kitchen drain tends to block because of a buildup of grease or soap, try pouring about one-quarter of a box of baking soda down it every month as a preventive measure.

**CLEANING THE EXTERIOR OF WHITE GOODS**

All exteriors of white goods, such as refrigerators, washing machines, and freezers, will benefit from a wipe over now and again with a cloth soaked in a solution of baking soda and warm water. Greasy marks and dust will quickly disappear.

**CLEANING THE REFRIGERATOR**

I've always used baking soda in solution to clean the inside of the refrigerator. For refrigerators that you had to turn off and defrost from time to time, I always wiped the trays and shelves with a strong solution. As well as cleaning up greasy marks it removes any odors from spills, milk bottle bottoms, and cheesy whiffs. With the larder fridge we have now, I remove any uncovered food, wipe down the shelves, and let dry as long as possible before replacing food items. Alternatively, wipe down with paper kitchen towel before putting the food back in.

If you are planning on turning off your refrigerator while you are away on a long vacation, or are moving house and need to leave it switched off for a while, using baking soda is a good way to save time and prevent mold from forming. I use it to clean out the fridge-freezer in our home in France when we leave each time, leaving the doors open and the power off. The only time we went back to black moldy deposits in the freezer was when a helpful workman closed the freezer door (to be fair, he did think he was doing us a favor) and I hadn't given the shelves the treatment. On return, a quick wipe over with a solution of baking soda in cold water was all that was needed before starting up the unit again.

Any stubborn stains that have sat at the back of the refrigerator for a while may be removed with a tablespoon of baking soda mixed with a squeeze of toothpaste.

### CLEANING THE OVEN INTERIOR

Even if your oven is really dirty you don't need to go to the desperate lengths of buying expensive and toxic oven cleaners. All you need is a thick paste of baking soda and water. Wipe over the inside when the oven has cooled down. Let stand overnight while the soda does its work. Wipe down with warm water to remove the grease and grot. Stubborn areas can be treated with straight baking soda on a scourer or cloth. You can clean a glass door with a weak solution, perhaps kept in a labeled spray bottle.

An alternative method is to spray the inside of the oven (once it is cool/cold) with water and place baking soda on the oven floor. Keep the oven moist by spraying every few hours and then let stand overnight before removing the deposits.

### CLEANING THE TOP OF THE STOVE

Wet the area and sprinkle baking soda onto the top. Let it sit for about 30 minutes before removing and rinsing off.

### COFFEEMAKERS

Running baking soda and water through the machine will give it a good clean and refresh it. Rinse with plenty of clear water afterward to remove all traces of the baking soda.

### DISHWASHERS

Baking soda will remove that nasty, crusty buildup you get on the inside of the door. Use as a paste and rinse off before running the machine. Try using baking soda instead of the usual powder or tablet once in a while to clean the dishwasher, too.

**DISHWASHER POWDER**

Instead of using a commercial brand of dishwashing detergent, try mixing two tablespoons of baking soda with two tablespoons of borax for a load.

**FREEZERS**

Another chance to use the solution is when the spare freezer in the garage has been off, or we've stored various family members' freezers etc. Cleaning with baking soda and warm water has always kept the units fresh—as long as the door is kept propped open.

If you defrost the freezer, wait for all the ice to melt, then wipe carefully with warm water solution and let it dry thoroughly. Restart the freezer . . . and close the door!

**GAS BURNERS**

If you can remove the gas burners easily to clean around them, immerse them in a pan of boiling water with four tablespoons of baking soda for a few minutes.

**GLASS AND STAINLESS STEEL COFFEEPOTS (not aluminum)**

Fill the pot or jug with warm water while it is standing in a sink. Add a dash of white vinegar and half a teaspoon of baking soda. Let it fizz and soak for a few minutes. Rinse with fresh water and dry carefully.

**MICROWAVES**

Use in solution to clean up food splatters on the bottom, sides, and ceiling. Remove the turntable plate and wipe over the interior, being careful not to let any water drip through the holes in the walls. The turntable can be cleaned with the same solution.

## POTS AND PANS WITH BAKED-ON DEPOSITS (NOTE: Not nonstick!)

1. For really burned-on grease and grime you can try the full assault. Remove what burned-on food you can, then pour a layer of baking soda onto the bottom of the pan and use just enough water to moisten the soda. Let stand until the next day, then scrub clean. Whenever I make custard the milk always burns on the bottom of the pan. This method makes cleaning a lot easier.

2. If that doesn't get it all off, for example, after a pan has been baking away in the oven for hours, put a layer of water in the bottom and add a cup of vinegar. Bring this to a boil, remove from the heat, and then sprinkle in two tablespoons of baking soda. Remember to expect the fizzing effect, and stand back unless you fancy the idea of two nostrils' full of the smell of vinegar at close quarters. The remains of the cooking should then loosen off without further resistance.

3. If the pan isn't too bad, soak it in baking soda and water for half an hour before washing normally. Alternatively, if you're not worried about scratching the pan, use the baking soda dry with a scouring pad.

4. Here's another idea: Mix one spoonful of salt with two of baking soda and mix with a little lemon juice. Spread this over the offending article and let dry. Rub off with a scouring pad.

## REFRESHING A VACUUM FLASK

To clean out an old vacuum flask add a teaspoon of baking soda and fill with warm water. Let steep for a while, then rinse out with cold water.

## REMOVING GREASE SPILLS

If you spill grease or oil on the kitchen floor while cooking, mop up what you can with paper towels, then sprinkle baking soda onto the spill. This can be mopped up later when you have more time, and will prevent the "skidding" that occurs if you use detergent straight away and which spreads across the floor.

**REMOVING HARD WATER STAINS**

Water stains are another common occurrence if you live in a hard water area. Use baking soda, sprinkled onto the stain, and then wipe clean with vinegar. Remember to watch out for the fizz!

**REMOVING NEWSPRINT STAINS FROM SURFACES**

Now this is one that I have experience of. The print can be a real pain to get rid of if you leave a newspaper lying on a slightly damp surface, or a drop of rain gets the paper wet before delivery. Make a paste with baking soda and a little water and rub gently until the stain disappears.

**REMOVING PLASTIC WRAPPERS FROM HOT SURFACES**

Have you ever caught a corner of a plastic bag wrapper of a loaf of bread on the toaster? Can't say I have, but it must be hard to get it off again. Dampen a cloth and make a mild scouring pad with some baking soda. Apparently, it will work well. Obviously you need to unplug electrical goods, such as toasters, before cleaning them like this and avoid getting any moisture on the inside element.

**REMOVING STAINS FROM COFFEE MUGS**

Sprinkle a little baking soda into the bottom of the cup and add warm water to make a paste. Let stand for a while before rinsing.

**REMOVING STAINS ON ENAMELED CAST-IRON WARE**

Most of my casseroles and saucepans are of the cast-iron variety, which are perfect for using on, and in, an old-fashioned oven (using minimal effort, with the same pot for cooking on top, inside the oven, or serving from at the table). The most loyal of these, given to me by my mother after many years of service with her, is now about 30 years old. The inside of the pot had become markedly browner than the original creamy color over the years, as a result of daily use and food stains (and regular burned-on food in the early days of cooking). It has been given a new lease of life by a treatment of baking soda and vinegar. Use Method 1, as above. Some of the newer pots won't get this treatment though, because they have a different, dark, nonstick coating.

### STAINLESS STEEL AND CHROME KITCHEN APPLIANCES

These can be polished with a moist cloth and baking soda. I tried it on our kettle, which stands on the stove top, but make sure the kettle is cool or empty first, otherwise the baking soda dries too quickly for you to polish the marks away.

### STAINLESS STEEL SINKS

Sometimes stainless steel can appear to be a misnomer, especially when tea and coffee dregs go down the sink. I regularly clean mine with a solution of vinegar and baking soda, as above.

An alternative to using vinegar with baking soda is to use club soda, which will avoid the possibility of scratching, especially on new sinks and appliances. If in doubt though, just use warm water.

### STEEL WOOL PAN SCRUBBERS

Despite the many other scourers available these days, some of us still like to use the old pads on stubborn stains to baking pans and cast iron. If you don't use them very often, keep them in a box with some dry baking soda powder and they won't go rusty.

### STUBBORN STAINS ON COUNTERTOPS

To remove stubborn stains from marble, plastic, or Formica, make a strong paste of baking soda with water. Scour gently and then rinse thoroughly.

## WASTE DISPOSAL UNITS

You can apparently clean waste disposal units out with a mixture of baking soda, lemon juice, and vinegar. I prefer composting my kitchen waste.

## COUNTERTOPS

Use baking soda on a damp cloth to clean countertops and leave them free of smells. You can sprinkle the powder directly onto a cloth or sponge, or make up a solution. Rinse with clean water and dry. The solution can be used to clean your cleaning cloths as well and to keep them smelling nice.

## GREEN BATHROOM USES

CLEANING BATHROOM TRAPS ..... 91
CLEANING OUT THE BATHTUB AND WASH BASIN ..... 91
CLEANING FAUCETS ..... 91
CLEANING THE TOILET BOWL ..... 91
CLEANING TILES AND GROUTING ..... 91
FLUSHING WITH SODA ..... 92
FRAGRANT SINK CLEANER ..... 92
GETTING RID OF DAMP UNDER THE BASIN ..... 92
REMOVING SOAP SCUM FROM THE SHOWER ..... 92
SHOWER CURTAINS ..... 93

Anywhere that water lurks there are likely to be odors and moldy deposits. Add a lack of air circulating, for example, in a bathroom or shower room, and the possibilities for using baking soda are endless it seems.

**CLEANING BATHROOM TRAPS**
If you have one of those removable traps in the shower, bathtub, or wash basin, you can remove it, along with the gross, slimy buildup of hair, shampoo, conditioner, gel, etc. that is so disgusting to deal with. Soak the removable part in a plastic bowl in a solution of baking soda and warm water. Add vinegar to make it more effective (use an old ice cream container, but make sure you throw it away or recycle it immediately afterwards).

**CLEANING OUT THE BATHTUB AND WASH BASIN**
Using the paste of two parts baking soda to one part vinegar, you can remove the built-up soap scum by gently applying with a damp cloth. Rinse with cold water. The drain hole will benefit as well.

**CLEANING FAUCETS**
Another gratifying job! While you have some of the paste mixed for the tiles, as above, give the bottom of the faucets a treat as well. I'd been trying to get the marks off where the basin meets the chrome for a while and had even bought a commercial product, which I didn't use when I saw the contents and read the cautions attached. The baking soda worked perfectly.

**CLEANING THE TOILET PAN**
Instead of using bleach, try putting baking soda down the toilet bowl. Let stand a while before flushing away. The toilet seat can be wiped with a baking soda solution as well.

**CLEANING TILES AND GROUTING**
This creates instant results and a sense of extreme satisfaction. Using an old toothbrush and a paste made of

two parts baking soda to one part white vinegar rids the grout of that yellowy pink look that builds up in the shower a little at a time. The initial smell of vinegar quickly disappears. Rinse with the showerhead for quick results.

### FLUSHING WITH SODA

Every month or so, sprinkle a little baking soda into the toilet tank and let stand overnight. Flush in the morning and you, too, will flush with pride!

### FRAGRANT SINK CLEANER

Put about four tablespoons of baking soda into a bowl with enough liquid soap to make a paste. Add a drop of tea tree oil, two drops of lemon oil, and two of orange or lavender oil.

### GETTING RID OF DAMP UNDER THE BASIN

Where cleaning cloths lurk, along with unwanted or half-used bottles of something you got for Christmas last year and the odd washcloth or old toothbrush, is the perfect place for nasty damp patches to form. Leave a box of baking soda with the lid off to absorb the damp.

### REMOVING SOAP SCUM FROM THE SHOWER

If you have a shower cubicle you will know how difficult it can be to get in all the corners and to clean the inside of the sliding doors properly. Try using a paste of baking soda and vinegar. Use four tablespoons of baking soda to two of vinegar. This can be applied to the doors with a cloth and you can use an old toothbrush to get into the corners. It will cut through the soap scum and refresh the darkest recesses. It also refreshes the drain hole and drain as a bonus.

**SHOWER CURTAINS**

I don't have these anymore, but remember vividly that unpleasant smell of old plastic with a trim of mold along the seams. Put them in the bathtub and brush or sponge with four or five tablespoons of baking soda. You can use an old toothbrush for the seams. Rinse with hot water and white vinegar. Hang the curtains—outside if possible—to dry thoroughly.

## GENERAL GREEN USES

ALUMINUM WINDOW AND DOOR FRAMES .................. 95
BRASS CLEANER 1 .................................................. 95
BRASS CLEANER 2 .................................................. 95
CARPET CLEANER .................................................. 95
CLEANING UP VOMIT .............................................. 95
CRAYON MARKS ...................................................... 95
FLOOR CLEANER...................................................... 96
HELPING TO PUT ON RUBBER GLOVES...................... 96
INK SPILLS ............................................................ 96
SILVER CLEANER 1.................................................. 96
SILVER CLEANER 2.................................................. 96
SPILLS ON BOOKS .................................................. 97
SUPER FILLER ...................................................... 97
VINYL CHAIRS ...................................................... 97

Remember, it's always a good idea to do a spot test in a hidden area on a surface if you haven't used the suggested methods before. If you have leftover solutions, make sure they are labeled and kept out of harm's way.

**ALUMINUM WINDOW AND DOOR FRAMES**
Mix two parts baking soda to one part vinegar for cleaning tracks, fittings, and frames. Wipe clean with a damp cloth.

**BRASS CLEANER 1**
A recipe I came across for cleaning brass suggests using two tablespoons of flour, one tablespoon of salt, and one tablespoon of baking soda mixed together with vinegar to make a thick paste.

**BRASS CLEANER 2**
Sprinkle some baking soda onto half a lemon and rub clean. Rinse and polish dry thoroughly.

**CARPET CLEANER**
Whatever the spill, use baking soda to soak up as much of the liquid as possible. This can then be swept up and the carpet dabbed with a mild solution of baking soda and warm water. Allow to dry thoroughly before vacuuming.

**CLEANING UP VOMIT**
My mom told me about this when our children were babies. It works really well on most floor surfaces. Use a solution of baking soda and water for mild cases and work into the carpet gradually. It kills the lingering smell, too.

**CRAYON MARKS**
These can be removed with a mild solution of baking soda and water, rinsed with hot water.

## FLOOR CLEANER

Use a solution of baking soda dissolved in warm water. Use as you would any other floor cleaner.

## HELPING TO PUT ON RUBBER GLOVES

This sounds like a good trick, only I always forget to put the gloves on before I start a messy job. After you have used the gloves, rinsing them before removal, sprinkle a little baking soda inside each one. It will help to get them on next time and will prevent any smell.

## INK SPILLS

These can be treated on a hard floor surface with baking soda-and-vinegar solution. Rub the stain gently until it fades.

## SILVER CLEANER 1

Silver can be cleaned with a paste of baking soda and water, which saves you using toxic chemicals again and also prevents your precious silver from being worn away. Use three tablespoonfuls of baking soda to one of warm water. Spread over the object and let it dry. You can use an old toothbrush to get into all the crevices. Polish with a soft, clean cloth.

## SILVER CLEANER 2

For heavily tarnished silver, try this method. The tarnish is silver sulfide and this can be restored without abrasive cleaners through a little alchemy. For large items, fill a plastic bucket with hot water and put a piece of aluminum foil in the bottom. Sprinkle baking soda over the item to be cleaned and put it into the water. Let it stand for 15 minutes before taking it out and drying with a soft cloth. Smaller items can be washed in an old aluminum foil baking tray in the same way. Magic!

(Well, okay, not really magic, but a reaction between aluminum, a very active metal, and silver, which is inert. Silver reacts with sulfur in the air, which makes it tarnish. The aluminum removes the sulfur by chemical reaction.)

**SPILLS ON BOOKS**

Horror of horrors, a spilled drink has spoiled your favorite book! Sprinkle baking soda on the wet pages and let them dry—in the sun if possible. Of course, if it's not your book, you'll have to confess (or, at least, come clean!).

**SUPER FILLER**

Apparently, you can mix baking soda with superglue to make a filler for cracks. Since I won't use the latter because of the smell and chemicals involved, I can't say I have any experience of this technique. Careful with that glue, though!

**VINYL CHAIRS**

Simply wipe down with a weak solution of baking soda and water. Follow this up with a dry cloth.

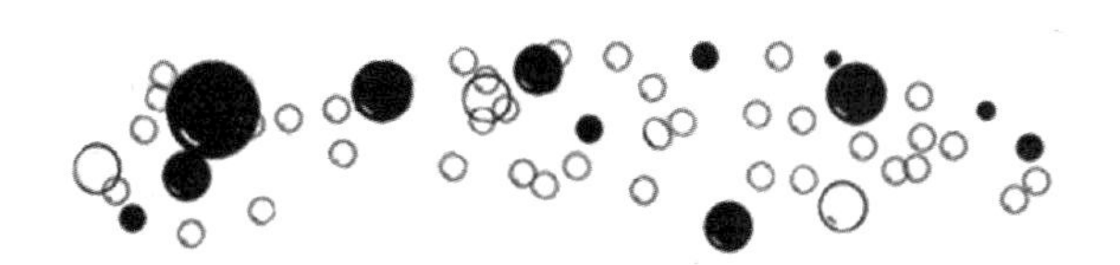

## GREEN LAUNDRY USES

CLEANING THE IRON ........................................ 99
FABRIC SOFTENER ........................................ 99
GREASE STAINS ........................................ 99
REMOVING BLOODSTAINS ........................................ 99
REMOVING MARKS ON SUEDE AND
UNWASHABLE FABRIC ITEMS ........................................ 99
REMOVING VOMIT ........................................ 99
SILK UNDERWEAR ........................................ 100
STAIN REMOVER ........................................ 100
WHITENER FOR WASHING ........................................ 100
WHITER DIAPERS WITH LESS EFFORT ........................................ 100

If in doubt about the color fastness of the item, or in the suitability of using baking soda on delicate fabrics, always try a small sample first on a less obvious part of the garment or item.

**CLEANING THE IRON**

Deposits on the bottom of an iron can be removed with a paste of baking soda and water. Unplug the iron first and let it cool down!

**FABRIC SOFTENER**

Added to the laundry, baking soda acts as a fabric softener. Mixing one part vinegar (white), one part baking soda, and two parts water will make a suitable solution, which you can keep in a bottle (labeled). Add four tablespoons to the final rinse.

**GREASE STAINS**

These can be removed before you wash the item with a paste of two parts baking soda to one part cream of tartar, mixed with a little water. Rub the grease mark gently before washing.

**REMOVING BLOODSTAINS**

Soak clothing in a bucket of cold water with a cup of vinegar and an equal amount of baking soda. Let stand overnight before washing as normal.

**REMOVING MARKS ON SUEDE AND UNWASHABLE FABRIC ITEMS**

Sprinkle baking soda over the item and brush gently to remove dirt and grease. Check a small part of the item that won't be obvious first.

**REMOVING VOMIT**

Soak as for removing bloodstains, but with double the baking soda, and without the vinegar.

## SILK UNDERWEAR

This has been recommended for use with silk underwear, when you don't want to use commercial fabric conditioners that may harm sensitive skin. Rinse the garments in a mild solution of baking soda and water every ten or so washes. This should remove any buildup of minerals without affecting the skin.

## STAIN REMOVER

Rinse the article in cold water before the stain dries. Apply baking soda to the stain and then wash as normal. Don't try this on delicate fabrics, such as silk (but see above for silk underwear treatment).

## WHITENER FOR WASHING

Mix one part lemon juice with one part baking soda. Add to your whites for a mild bleaching effect.

## WHITER DIAPERS WITH LESS EFFORT

If cloth diapers make the comeback they deserve, to save using valuable resources, then this will help. Soak the diapers in a bucket of baking soda solution overnight. When you wash them, you won't need so much laundry detergent or much hot water to keep them white.

## GREEN OUTDOOR USES

BARBECUE GRILLS .......... 102
BATTERY ACID SPILL AND CLEANER .......... 102
BLACK SPOT PREVENTIVE .......... 102
DEALING WITH GREASE OR OIL SPILLS .......... 102
DOORMATS .......... 102
GARBAGE CANS .......... 102
FIRE PREVENTION .......... 103
GARDEN FURNITURE .......... 103
GREENHOUSES .......... 103
MELTING SNOW AND ICE .......... 103
OUTSIDE DRAINS .......... 103
PADDLING POOLS .......... 103
PAINTBRUSH RESTORER .......... 104
REGULATING THE pH IN A POOL OR SPA .......... 104
SEPTIC TANKS .......... 104
SPA BATHS AND POOL AREAS .......... 104
SPRAYING AGAINST POWDERY MILDEW .......... 104
TEST FOR SOIL ACIDITY .......... 104
WASHING BUGS OFF THE CAR .......... 105
WINDSHIELDS AND WINDOWS .......... 105

### BARBECUE GRILLS

These get a lot of abuse. Sometimes the grease and dirt can be burned off by the next barbecue, especially if these are a frequent summer occurrence. More often than not, rain stops play in our yard (we are famous for wet barbies). A scrub with baking soda and vinegar will clean up the mess, even after the rain.

### BATTERY ACID SPILL AND CLEANER

Sprinkle baking soda onto battery acid spills to neutralize the acid. You can clean battery terminals with two teaspoons of baking soda mixed with 4 cups (1 liter) of water. Smearing a little petroleum jelly around the bottom of the terminal will help prevent further problems.

### BLACK SPOT PREVENTIVE

Use the spray above, but add a drop of vegetable oil to the bottle to help the mixture stick to the leaves when dried. The soap helps to spread the mixture and the baking soda makes the surfaces of the leaves alkaline, which will inhibit the fungal spores. The biggest advantage of this is that there will be no adverse environmental impact because the ingredients are safe.

### DEALING WITH GREASE OR OIL SPILLS

If you have grease or oil spilled on the garage floor, sprinkle with baking soda and let it stand. Brush up and rinse.

### DOORMATS

Porch and outside doormats can be cleaned with a sprinkling of baking soda. Brush vigorously and then sweep away the dirt. Next time it rains the job will be complete.

### GARBAGE CANS

Sprinkle half a box of baking soda into the bottom of the empty garbage can. Swill around with a couple of bowls of warm water and let stand for a while. Empty out down the nearest drain.

**FIRE PREVENTION**

Because baking soda creates carbon dioxide, it is a useful substance to have around where there are flammable chemicals or grease. The soda will prevent oxygen from feeding the flames. Keep a box handy.

**GARDEN FURNITURE**

Wipe down with a solution of water and baking soda at the end of the winter to clean and freshen the table and chairs.

**GREENHOUSES**

Our old greenhouse gets musty if there isn't enough ventilation. Ever since water got through the roof we've had a hard time getting the wood dried out and the air freshened in the winter months. Half a box of baking soda left open absorbs some of the damp smell and creates carbon dioxide for the plants. You can also wash down the interior with a solution of baking soda and water to inhibit spores and bacteria.

**MELTING SNOW AND ICE**

Instead of using salt on the garden path, which will harm any plants it comes into contact with, use baking soda to melt snow and ice.

**OUTSIDE DRAINS**

1. Outside drains need some care as well. Use half a box of baking soda and a cup of vinegar. Stand back as the fizz works its magic. Leave this for an hour or two, then pour down a lot of very hot water.
2. You can also use equal quantities of salt and baking soda with some boiling water.

**PADDLING POOLS**

Children's paddling pools can be cleaned with a solution of baking soda and water. At the end of the season repeat this method and allow the paddling pool to dry thoroughly before putting away in storage.

## PAINTBRUSH RESTORER

You may be able to salvage your old paintbrushes that have become hard by soaking them in 2 cups (475 ml) of hot water with two tablespoons of vinegar and four of baking soda. This won't work on brushes used for oil-based paint that you didn't clean with mineral spirits, but will renovate brushes used for water-based paints.

## REGULATING THE pH IN A POOL OR SPA

When alkalinity needs to be increased in swimming pools and spas, baking soda can be added to restore a balance if there is too much chlorine.

## SEPTIC TANKS

Adding a box of baking soda to a septic tank will maintain a healthy pH and keep an environment just right for bacteria to do their job. I'm still glad that we have municipal drainage now, though!

## SPA BATHS AND POOL AREAS

Use a solution of baking soda and water to wash down the walkways.

## SPRAYING AGAINST POWDERY MILDEW

This is an old treatment to prevent plants suffering from mildew. It is also a lot safer to use than harsh chemicals, especially if you are trying to be organic. Before spraying, first water the foliage and let it dry. Spray in the evening and never in full sunlight, otherwise the leaves will probably get scorched.

Mix together half a tablespoon of baking soda with 2 cups (475 ml) of soapy water in a spray bottle. Apply to both sides of the leaves of plants normally affected.

## TEST FOR SOIL ACIDITY

Use baking soda in the garden to test for acidity. If the soil bubbles it is too acidic and will need neutralizing.

### WASHING BUGS OFF THE CAR
Use a solution to wash the car and remove dead insects. Use on the windshield to remove grease and a buildup of dirt.

### WINDSHIELDS AND WINDOWS
These can be cleaned with a damp cloth sprinkled with a little baking soda. I still like vinegar for the job, myself.

## PETS AND PESTS

CLEANING OUT A FISH TANK ................................ 107
CLEARING UP SOMETHING THE CAT BROUGHT UP ...... 107
COCKROACHES ................................................ 107
DOG BATH AND FLEA CONTROL ............................ 107
RIDDING YOUR HOUSE OF ANTS ............................ 107

### CLEANING OUT A FISH TANK

Having removed fish, water, and other contents, use a thick paste of baking soda and white vinegar to remove stains and smells. Rinse thoroughly before reintroducing the fish.

### CLEARING UP SOMETHING THE CAT BROUGHT UP

Using baking soda in water is a great way to wipe over surfaces where the cat has parked his lunch or left his calling card. As with carpet cleaning and other floor surfaces, it removes the stain and takes the smell away, too.

### COCKROACHES

Luckily, I've never had to deal with these, but apparently mixing equal parts of baking soda with sugar and spreading where they lurk, such as dark, dank, undersink areas and behind baseboards, will keep them away.

### DOG BATH AND FLEA CONTROL

Adding a little white vinegar and baking soda to a bath will make your dog less doggy and also leave a soft coat. Some suggestions I've come across advise sprinkling baking soda directly onto the dog's coat, but I'm not a dog owner and it sounds like something of a trial to me—for the dog and the owner. If left in contact for long, the soda might harm the dog's skin, so the bath seems a kinder and simpler way.

Sprinkling into the dog's coat and combing out sounds like a dry shampoo treatment.

### RIDDING YOUR HOUSE OF ANTS

Put some baking soda inside the bottom of the door frame to drive away ants. Once they get in the house they are a real pain.

## NEUTRALIZING NASTY SMELLS

AIR FRESHENER FOR CARPETS ..... 109
AIR FRESHENER FOR THE ROOM ..... 109
ATTICS AND BASEMENTS ..... 109
DEODORIZING CARPETS IN THE CAR ..... 109
DEODORIZING DISUSED FLASKS ..... 109
DEODORIZING CLOTH DIAPERS ..... 109
DEODORIZING THE TRASH CAN ..... 110
DEODORIZING WOODEN CUTTING BOARDS ..... 110
DRAINS AGAIN ..... 110
REFRIGERATOR DEODORIZER ..... 110
GETTING RID OF A WOODY SMELL ..... 110
GETTING RID OF ODORS ON YOUR HANDS ..... 110
GREENHOUSE MUSTINESS ..... 110
"HANG ANYWHERE" DEODORIZING SACHETS ..... 111
MUSTY MATTRESSES ..... 111
NO-SMELL KITTY LITTER ..... 111
PILLOWS ..... 111
SMELLY SHOES ..... 111
SMELLY SWIMMING BAGS ..... 111
NICER SMELLING RUBBER GLOVES ..... 112
UNDERSINK ODOR ..... 112
VACUUM CLEANER TREAT ..... 112

**AIR FRESHENER FOR CARPETS**
Equal proportions of baking soda and cornstarch can be sprinkled on a smelly carpet or rug at night. In the morning, vacuum up the powder and the whiff should be gone.

**AIR FRESHENER FOR THE ROOM**
Mix a few drops of preferred oil fragrance with a small bowl of baking soda. This is much cheaper than a commercial air freshener, without any cloying or overpowering fragrance. You could even use an ashtray, thereby indicating that smoking is not encouraged in the house!

**ATTICS AND BASEMENTS**
Again, open containers of baking soda will act as air fresheners in areas you don't visit very often, like the attic.

**DEODORIZING CARPETS IN THE CAR**
Our car used to smell of old dog, even though we didn't have one (a dog, that is!). We had a mystery problem with a leaky seal (no, not the kind that can perform circus tricks!). Putting baking soda into the unused ashtray would have solved the problem. Alas, the car was written off in an accident before I could put it to the test. Alternatively, I would also have tried sprinkling baking soda onto the carpets before vacuuming.

**DEODORIZING DISUSED FLASKS**
As well as cleaning, a solution of baking soda and water will refresh the inside of the flask and eliminate any residual smell.

**DEODORIZING CLOTH DIAPERS**
I know that most parents seem to use disposable diapers nowadays, but they weren't an option when my kids were babies. Soaking diapers in a bucket with a solution of baking soda and water overnight was a ritual that not only got rid of the smell of ammonia but also cut down

the amount of laundry detergent needed to keep them white and stain free. I can't recall the children ever suffering from diaper rash either.

### DEODORIZING THE TRASH CAN

Sprinkle baking soda in your trash can to keep the smell down in hot weather.

### DEODORIZING WOODEN CUTTING BOARDS

The smell of onions etc. can be eradicated by wiping the board with a solution of baking soda and warm water.

### DRAINS AGAIN

Yes, as well as cutting through the grease, the baking soda will deodorize your drains.

### REFRIGERATOR DEODORIZER

You can do this by either wiping out the refrigerator with a cloth washed in a baking soda solution, or by leaving a small opened box of the powder inside.

### GETTING RID OF A WOODY SMELL

If you don't like the smell that emanates from that old wooden chest or wardrobe, try sprinkling a little baking soda in the bottom and covering it with lining paper. Alternatively, place an opened box of the powder in the bottom. Don't forget it is there, though—you might end up knocking it over!

### GETTING RID OF ODORS ON YOUR HANDS

A great way to get rid of the smell of fish on your hands is to rub them with baking soda before washing them.

### GREENHOUSE MUSTINESS

The use of an open, half box of baking soda will freshen the air during the months when you can't have the windows open.

### "HANG ANYWHERE" DEODORIZING SACHETS

This recycling trick might be useful and mean that you don't have bowls of white powder lying around everywhere. Use the foot of an old stocking or pair of panty hose to make a deodorizing sachet that you can hang anywhere. Put the baking soda into the foot, twist the leg around a few times, and go back over the ball of powder with a second layer of panty hose or stocking. This can be tied with a string, ribbon, rubber band, or whatever grabs you, and hung in a cupboard, hidden in the dog basket, or attic.

### MUSTY MATTRESSES

If the house, or spare room, has been shut up for a while and not properly aired, the mattress may smell a bit damp and musty, even if it is perfectly dry. Turn the mattress and sprinkle a little baking soda on before you make up the bed with fresh bedding.

### NO-SMELL KITTY LITTER

Sprinkling a little baking soda into the litter tray when washing out or changing the contents, will deodorize the tray.

### PILLOWS

If your pillows are liable to smell and you can't give them a good airing outside, put a little dry baking soda inside with the filling to keep them smelling fresh.

### SMELLY SHOES

The worst smell in the world comes wafting out of my son's sneakers. Sprinkling baking soda into them—if he leaves them here again—will be an undiluted pleasure!

### SMELLY SWIMMING BAGS

These can be freshened with a sprinkling of baking soda.

## NICER SMELLING RUBBER GLOVES

After you have used the gloves, rinsing them before removal, sprinkle a little baking soda inside each one. It will help to prevent any smell coming from them when you use them next time.

## UNDERSINK ODOR

Place an open container of baking soda on the shelf under the sink to avoid nasty smells from cloths and cleaning paraphernalia. Of course, if you rinse out the cloths in baking soda, they won't smell anyway.

## VACUUM CLEANER TREAT

Sprinkling a little powder into the new bag will stop that old dog smell, especially if you don't need to change the bag very often.

## MISCELLANEOUS GREEN USES

BATHWATER SOFTENER .................................... 114
BEE STINGS .................................... 114
BRUSHES AND COMBS .................................... 114
CLEANING CONTACT LENSES .................................... 114
CLEANING SKIN ABRASIONS .................................... 114
COLD SORES .................................... 114
DRY SHAMPOO 1 .................................... 115
DRY SHAMPOO 2 .................................... 115
DRY SKIN TREATMENT .................................... 115
FACE WASH .................................... 115
FOOT ODOR EATER .................................... 115
GARGLING AND MOUTHWASH .................................... 115
GUM MASSAGE .................................... 116
HAND TREATMENT .................................... 116
RELIEVING ACID INDIGESTION .................................... 116
RELIEVING ACIDITY IN URINE .................................... 117
RELIEVING INSECT BITES .................................... 117
RELIEVING MILD SKIN INFECTIONS .................................... 117
RELIEVING SKIN IRRITATION .................................... 117
REMOVING A BUILDUP OF HAIR PRODUCTS .................................... 117
REMOVING SPLINTERS .................................... 118
SUNBURN .................................... 118
TOOTH WHITENER AND CLEANER .................................... 118
TOOTHBRUSH CARE .................................... 118
UNDERARM DEODORANT .................................... 118
WART TREATMENT .................................... 118

My research has led me to some interesting solutions to old problems as well as some truly bizarre ones. I've put in some of the old, natural remedies for interest rather than to recommend them. Obviously, these are suggestions only and if you have any doubts, consult your doctor or a specialist in the field before launching in.

### BATHWATER SOFTENER

Use half a cup of baking soda in the bathtub, and add to running water.

### BEE STINGS

Mix a paste of baking soda and water. Apply to the swelling after the sting has been removed.

### BRUSHES AND COMBS

These can be cleaned in a solution of baking soda and warm water to remove a buildup of products. If you can, immerse the whole brush. If you are worried about harming the handle of a top-quality model or an antique, bristle variety, you can swish the bristles around in the water without immersing the whole thing. This was how the Victorians washed pure bristle brushes.

### CLEANING CONTACT LENSES

Apparently, baking soda in water cleans contact lenses. You must rinse very thoroughly, however, to avoid stinging.

### CLEANING SKIN ABRASIONS

Wash with a mild solution of baking soda and warm water.That sounds fine, but what about sprinkling the graze with black pepper while still wet? I leave that part of the remedy entirely up to you.

### COLD SORES

Apply the baking soda as a paste with water onto the sore, but don't rub. This will promote healing as well as soothing the affected area.

## DRY SHAMPOO 1

I remember someone at school doing this with talcum powder when I was a teenager because everyone was obsessed with not having greasy hair. I can't think of when there isn't time to wash your hair nowadays in the shower, apart from when camping and/or faced with a lack of water. However, the tip is sprinkle baking soda onto your hair and rub through. Comb out and dry in warm air. Luckily, I don't have greasy hair anymore!

## DRY SHAMPOO 2

This sounds even less pleasant. Sprinkle one teaspoon of oatmeal and one of baking soda on your head. Massage in for a few minutes, then comb or brush out. Again, warm air will help to get rid of residue.

## DRY SKIN TREATMENT

Make a paste of baking soda and olive oil. Apply to dry skin, for example, rough elbows, and let stand for three minutes. Rinse with warm water.

## FACE WASH

A mild solution of baking soda in warm water is good for washing your face without soap. It will also help to clean the pores and may prevent acne.

## FOOT ODOR EATER

Use baking soda as a substitute for talcum powder after washing your feet. See below for a foot spa suggestion.

## FOOT SPA

To put life and harmony back into tired, smelly feet, soak them in a bowl of hot water with four tablespoons of baking soda. Bliss! The soaking will also soften hard skin, which you can remove with a pumice stone.

## GARGLING AND MOUTHWASH

Gargling with half a teaspoon of baking soda in a small glass of water will freshen and soothe your mouth and throat.

## GUM MASSAGE

Slightly more astringent, but a powerful gum massage: Take equal amounts of baking soda and salt. Rub this into your gums with your finger.

Alternatively, sprinkle half a teaspoon of baking soda onto your toothbrush and brush as normal.

## HAND TREATMENT

To soften hands, put two tablespoons of baking soda into a bowl of hot water. Sit and soak your hands for about 20 minutes. Dry them and apply hand cream, then place your hands inside clean cotton gloves or clean socks for another 20 minutes and relax. Of course, if you use the socks, you might have a bit of explaining to do, which may also cause you to laugh a lot, but laughing is good for you, too! In which case, don't try the next item at the same time.

## RELIEVING ACID INDIGESTION

This age-old remedy has given relief to generations. baking soda is used in the manufacture of several commercial brands, including Alka-Seltzer and Andrews Liver Salts.

## CAUTION

There may be several causes for prolonged indigestion, so you should consult your doctor if the symptoms persist. Also, if you are taking medication, you should check that the baking soda does not interfere with other treatment and, if you have heart problems or high blood pressure, you need to limit your intake of sodium. Obviously this remedy would be adding extra sodium. Taking baking soda for indigestion should be considered as a temporary solution or for an occasional problem and you should never take indigestion remedies for more than two weeks at a time.

***Children under six should never be given baking soda for indigestion.***

'he normal dose for adults is half a teaspoon in water every two hours. Avoid taking large quantities of milk or nilk products. Children from 6 to 12 years can be given quarter to half a teaspoonful in water after meals.

**RELIEVING ACIDITY IN URINE**

As already stated above, this is not a long-term solution. Baking soda makes urine less acidic. Uric acid can lead to idney stone formation, so check with your doctor if in doubt.

Take one teaspoon in water every four hours. Do not take more than four doses a day. Remember also that this will increase your sodium intake a lot, so beware if you have high blood pressure.

**RELIEVING INSECT BITES**

Apply a paste of baking soda and water to the affected area. This should relieve the irritation or discomfort.

**RELIEVING MILD SKIN INFECTIONS**

Some of these suggestions date back centuries. I offer them for interest.

Make a poultice as follows. Slice two onions finely and cook until tender in 2 cups (475 ml) of water. Thicken with wheat bran and add half a tablespoon of baking soda. Put this poultice on the affected area and change as often as is necessary to reduce inflammation.

**RELIEVING SKIN IRRITATION**

If you have a skin irritation, or are getting over chicken pox, try adding three tablespoons of baking soda to a warm bath.

**REMOVING A BUILDUP OF HAIR PRODUCTS**

If you have been using a lot of hair products, you can get rid of the buildup by mixing two tablespoons of baking soda with a tablespoon of shampoo. Massage this into your hair while you are washing it and rinse thoroughly. Don't put anything else on right away, such as conditioner, which you probably don't need anyway.

### REMOVING SPLINTERS

Mix a little water with half a teaspoon of baking soda to form a paste. Apply this to a splinter and cover it with a bandaid for a couple of hours. The soda should draw out the splinter, which can then be easily removed, along with any toxins, and solve the problem.

### SUNBURN

Relieve sunburn by making a paste of baking soda and water and spreading over the affected area. You can also try this if you have a poison ivy rash. Alternatively, put 1 cup (225 ml) of baking soda into a tepid bath for relief and soothing.

### TOOTH WHITENER AND CLEANER

After brushing with toothpaste, apply a little baking soda to the toothbrush and rebrush your teeth. This will help to whiten them.

### TOOTHBRUSH CARE

This may be useful when camping or traveling. Clean your toothbrush with a little sprinkle of baking soda and rinse in water.

### UNDERARM DEODORANT

Dust the armpits with baking soda after washing or showering.

### WART TREATMENT

Apply a few drops of vinegar to the wart and dust with baking soda. Remove after 15 minutes. Repeat several times a day, until the wart disappears.

# LEMONS

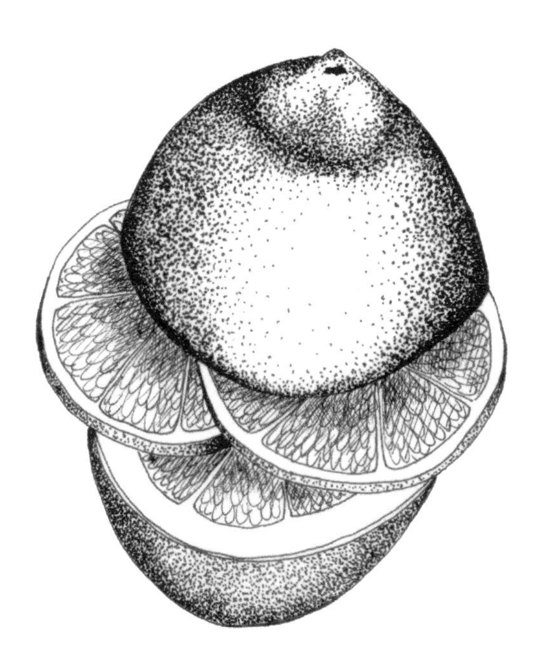

# WHY USE LEMONS?

*Lemon tree very pretty and the lemon flower is sweet but the fruit of the poor lemon is impossible to eat.*

THE LEMON TREE by Will Holt

Lemon juice is nature's natural bleach and disinfectant rolled into one. Not only is it an efficient stain remover but also a great deodorizer, making it a very efficient and harmless cleaner.

The first lemon groves were cultivated along the Italian Amalfi Coast in the year AD 200, where the climate was perfect for fruiting. Even as far back as AD 1200 lemons were prized for their medicinal qualities. They were introduced into Assyria, where they were discovered by soldiers serving Alexander the Great, who then took them back to Greece. The Arabs were largely responsible for the cultivation of lemons in the Mediterranean region. In addition to the Mediterranean, the fruit flourished in Sicily, Spain, and parts of northern Africa, which are still the main producers of lemons for Europe.

The lemon reached America through Columbus during his second voyage and since 1950, California has produced more lemons than all of Europe combined.

Lemons have the highest Vitamin C content of any of the citrus fruits and the juice of just one fruit provides 35 percent of the daily requirement. Lemon juice also helps to stimulate the development of white corpuscles, improving the body's ability to defend itself against infection.

Not only is it the best antiscorbutic (or remedy for scurvy) it is also known to counteract the effects of narcotics, soothe sunburn, cure jaundice, and reduce

emperature. Added to this, because of its high citric
cid content, it is perfect for preserving and stopping
ther fruit from going brown.

or many people, the scent of lemons symbolizes
reshness and cleanliness. In fact, many proprietary
leaning products have a lemon fragrance and so it makes
ense to use the versatile lemon in your daily cleaning
outine. When used as a cleaner, lemons are both
ntibacterial and antiseptic, making them a powerful
gent against germs and bacteria.

hey are also beneficial in the sense they are
iodegradable and safe for the environment, another
eason to choose lemons over many of the chemical
leaners found in stores today. Choose your fruit
arefully, only picking lemons that are firm to the touch,
voiding any that have obvious brown or soft spots.
emons with a greenish skin have not yet reached their
eak, and will not offer the benefits of a ripe fruit. So
emember to keep some lemons in your fruit bowl or
efrigerator and a bottle of freshly squeezed lemon juice
or convenience, too. Whole lemons will keep for up to
en days in a plastic bag in the refrigerator, although they
nay well last much longer. You can usually tell when a
emon is reaching the end of its storage life as the skin
ecomes more pitted and it starts to shrivel.

## ASCINATING FACTS

Believe it or not, lemons haven't always been thought of
o highly. At one time their yellow color was associated
vith infamy. Catalan priests banished the lemon,
elieving that it was the "fruit of the devil" because it
vasn't perfectly round like the orange and was deemed
o be deformed by the hands of Satan himself.

/irgil, however, told a different story. He believed that
he lemon had protective powers against all evil spirits:

"The sour apple with the persistent flavor is
an unrivaled remedy when cruel stepmothers
have poisoned a drink."

Casanova not only thought that the lemon was a miraculous aphrodisiac, he also used the juice as a form of contraception. In fact, lemon juice was commonly used in medieval times to prevent unwanted pregnancy.

## VARIETIES OF LEMONS

Lemons come in a variety of shapes and sizes. They can be large, small, thin- or thick-skinned, which can be either very smooth or extremely knobbly. There are 47 known varieties of lemons, broken down into two basic types: acid and sweet. The acid types are the ones that are more commercially available, recognized by their bright yellow color, good texture, and higher juice yield.

Some common varieties of lemons include:

**Baboon** is an oval fruit that has a tapered neck, which originated in Brazil. It has an intense yellow color to both its rind and heavily seeded flesh. It is very acidic, with a taste that is very similar to lime.

**Bearss**, is a Sicilian lemon with a rich and aromatic flavor similar to that of the Lisbon. The pulp is particularly firm and meaty and is also a commercial favorite in Florida.

**Escondido** is found near the Escondido River in Nicaragua. It has a thick rind, which is deep yellow in color and very oily. Although it is a small variety, it can still yield as much juice as some of the larger varieties.

**Eureka** lemon is probably the most widely grown lemon variety in the world. It has a high juice content, is thin-skinned, and is virtually seedless. It has a distinctive hort neck at the stem end and a pointed nipple at the lossom end.

**ino** is believed to be an old Spanish variety of lemon, vhich is mainly grown in Australia. The fruit is of good uality, juicy with a thin rind and high acidity levels.

**.isbon** lemon is another quality lemon with a high juice :ontent and thin skin, but it does not taper at the neck ike the Eureka. It is medium-sized elliptical in shape, vith a deep yellow, smooth rind. The flesh is a very pale ellow and seedless.

**Aeyer** ia a popular variety of lemon, although it is not a rue lemon. It is a natural hybrid between a lemon and either an orange or a mandarin. It has a lower acidity, educed bitterness, and a softer texture.

**/erna** is another lemon variety that has recently been ntroduced into Australia. The fruit are less rounded in shape than some other varieties, have a pronounced neck, and minimal seeds.

**/olkamer** is a hybrid of a lemon and a sour orange that originated in italy. It is small and round, with some seeds, and its quality equals a rough lemon. However, it does lack the quantity of juice and has a much lower level of acidity than most lemons.

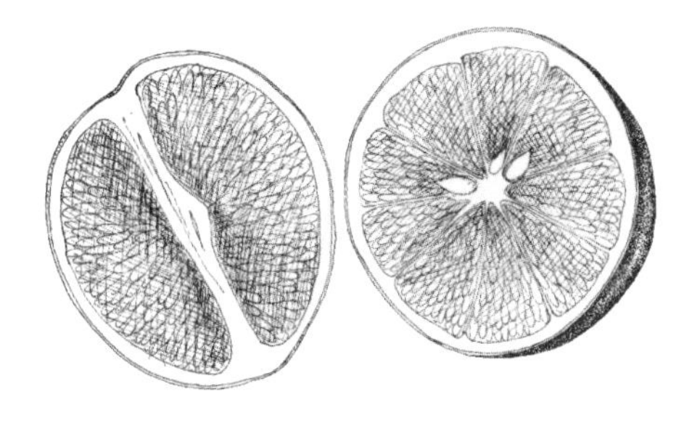

# THE USEFUL LEMON

Just like vinegar and baking soda, lemons are a cheap, natural cleaning product. The household uses for lemons go much further than just using them in cooking. Remember, lemons provide both antibacterial and antiseptic qualities, making them ideal for cleaning. Not only do they have a really refreshing smell, but lemons are able to cope with even those toughest cleaning jobs. Lemon juice is also a natural bleach, so adding it to your wash cycle not only gives you fresh smelling laundry, but also helps to brighten those whites as well.

Lemons are powerful enough to dissolve soap scum and even hard water deposits, and they are ideal for cleaning around the difficult bends of your kitchen and bathroom faucets. They also neutralize many odors and you can make a wonderful, natural air freshener by just mixing lemon juice and water in a spray bottle.

So next time you go to your cabinet and reach for one of the proprietary brands of cleaners, stop and think and consider the alternatives. Not only will you be helping the environment, but you are also being kind to your own body and skin.

# Green Cleaning Solutions with Lemons

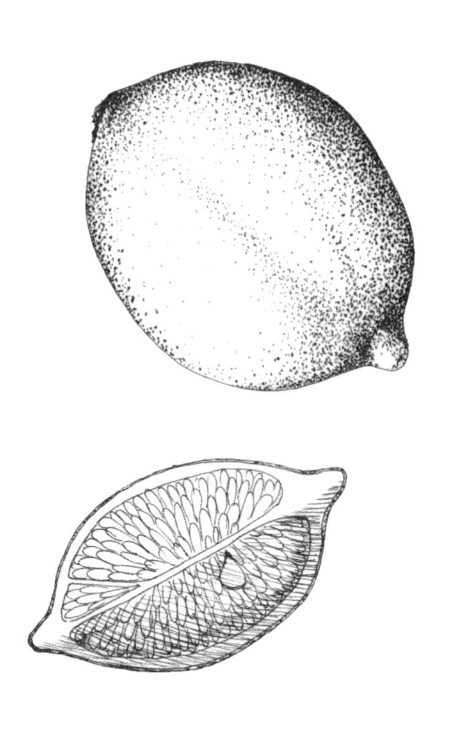

## GREEN KITCHEN USES

ALUMINUM........................................................ 127
ANTS ............................................................ 127
BURNED-ON FOOD .............................................. 127
BUTTERMILK .................................................. 127
CUTTING BOARDS ............................................ 127
DISHWASHER .................................................. 127
REFRIGERATOR FRESHENER.................................. 128
GLASS POTS.................................................... 128
KITCHEN TIPS.................................................. 128
MICROWAVE .................................................... 128
PORCELAIN ..................................................... 128
TUPPERWARE .................................................. 129
WASTE DISPOSAL .............................................. 129
WILTING LETTUCE ............................................ 129
COUNTERTOPS ................................................ 129

**ALUMINUM**
Brighten dull aluminum pots and pans by rubbing the cut side of a lemon all over them and buff with a soft cloth.

**ANTS**
If you want to antproof your kitchen just give them the lemon treatment. Squeeze lemon juice on door thresholds and windowsills and into any holes or cracks where ants are likely to get in. Finally, scatter some slices of lemon peel around the outdoor entrance. The ants will soon get the message that they are not welcome.

**BURNED-ON FOOD**
To remove stubborn burned-on food from a pan, fill it with warm water, add lemon slices, and allow it to simmer for about 15 minutes, or until the food starts to break loose from the surface.

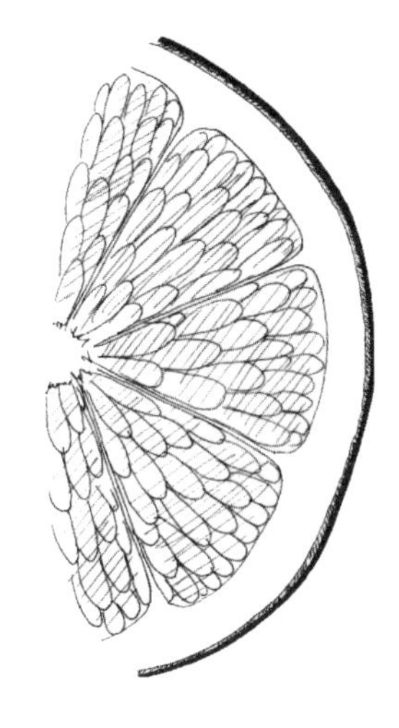

**BUTTERMILK**
Do you need buttermilk for a recipe but don't have any handy? Don't panic, just mix 1 cup (125 ml) of milk with a tablespoon of lemon juice for a substitute that tastes just as good.

**CUTTING BOARDS**
To get rid of the smell and help sanitize a cutting board (wooden or plastic), rub it all over with the cut side of half a lemon or wash it in undiluted lemon juice.

**DISHWASHER**
To sanitize your dishwasher and remove any unwanted mineral deposits and smells, make sure the machine is empty and then place lemon juice in the soap dispenser

and run through your normal wash cycle. Your dishwasher will not only be clean but will smell nice as well.

### REFRIGERATOR FRESHENER

Dab lemon juice onto a piece of cotton wool or sponge and put it in the refrigerator for several hours or overnight.

### GLASS POTS

Pour in lemon juice, add a generous amount of salt or baking soda and scrub with a brush or sponge.
For tough stains, let the mixture set, then scrub.

### KITCHEN TIPS

- A lemon at room temperature will yield more juice.
- Before juicing, press down firmly and roll the lemon on the countertop to help break up the pulp.
- Freeze lemon juice in ice cube trays and when frozen place in plastic bags.
- Grate lemon zest and seal tightly in plastic bags before freezing.
- Tenderize meat by marinating in lemon juice.
- Squeeze lemon on vegetables while steaming to help keep the colors bright.
- Add lemon juice to rice while it is cooking for a nice fluffy finish.
- A few drops of lemon juice will help improve the flavor of other fruits.

### MICROWAVE

To clean your microwave, mix 3 tablespoons of lemon juice into 1¾ cups (400 ml) of water in a microwave-safe pitcher or bowl. Microwave on High for 5 to 10 minutes, allowing the steam to condense on the inside of the microwave. Then simply wipe away the residue food with a cloth.

## PORCELAIN

If you have a stain on porcelain sink, pour lemon juice over the stain and then sprinkle with alum power (available in the spice aisle of your grocery store) and work into the stain thoroughly. If the stain doesn't come out immediately, leave the solution on overnight, then add more lemon juice, scrub, and rinse.

## TUPPERWARE

If your Tupperware or other plastic containers have become contaminated or stained, squeeze some lemon juice into the container and then add some baking soda. Use the lemon as a cleaning tool and work it in. If the stains are particularly bad, you can let it sit overnight before you scrub the stains.

## WASTE DISPOSAL

If your waste disposal is starting to whiff, here is an easy way to deodorize it. Save leftover lemon and orange peel and just toss them down the drain. To keep it smelling pleasant repeat this process once a month.

## WILTING LETTUCE

If your lettuce is looking a little wilted, place it in a bowl of water with 4 tablespoons of lemon juice. Put the bowl in the refrigerator and chill until you are ready to use it.

## COUNTERTOPS

We all know that countertops stain easily, but these can be removed by allowing lemon juice to sit on the stain for a few minutes. Then scrub the area with baking soda and watch the stains disappear. Remember, don't leave the lemon juice on the mark for too long, because it has a very powerful bleaching action.

## IN THE BATHROOM

AIR FRESHENER ........ 131
BATHTUB RINGS ........ 131
GROUT ........ 131
MIRRORS ........ 131
SHOWER DOORS ........ 131
FAUCETS ........ 131
TOILET BOWLS ........ 131

**AIR FRESHENER**
For a nice fresh smell in your bathroom, cut a lemon in half and leave it cut-side up in a small bowl on your windowsill.

**BATHTUB RINGS**
Treat bathtub rings by wiping them with lemon juice and then rub with a sponge.

**GROUT**
To brighten dull grout around your tiles, apply lemon juice with a toothbrush and scrub. Rinse with clean water.

MIRRORS
Using a solution of lemon juice and water, spray the mirror and then wipe dry with newspaper for a flawless finish.

**SHOWER DOORS**
To clean glass shower doors, apply lemon juice with a sponge. Dry with newspapers for a sparkling shine.

**FAUCETS**
Faucets can easily appear dirty because water deposits collect around these areas. To dissolve this, soak some paper towel in lemon juice and wrap it around the faucet, allowing about an hour to loosen the alkaline. Then scrub the tap with a stiff toothbrush.

**TOILET BOWLS**
For stains around your toilet bowl, mix a paste to about the consistency of toothpaste, using borax and lemon juice. Apply the paste to the sides of your toilet and leave it for two hours or longer. Scrub the surface thoroughly and rinse.

## IN THE LAUNDRY

BLEACHING .................................................... 133
BOOST LAUNDRY DETERGENT .............................. 133
BRIGHTEN WHITES.............................................. 133
INK STAINS .................................................... 133
RASPBERRY AND RED CURRANT STAINS.................... 133
RUST STAINS .................................................. 133
STAINS ON WHITE CLOTHING................................ 134
STUBBORN STAINS ............................................ 134
WHITE SOCKS.................................................. 134

**BLEACHING**
Lemon juice acts as a natural bleaching agent, so put some lemon juice onto white linens and clothing and allow them to dry in natural sunlight. Those stains will soon be bleached away. (DO NOT USE THIS SOLUTION ON SILK.)

**BOOST LAUNDRY DETERGENT**
To remove discolorations from cotton T-shirts and underpants, pour 1 cup (225 ml ) lemon juice into the washing machine during the wash cycle. The natural bleaching action of the juice will zap the stains and leave the clothes smelling fresh.

**BRIGHTEN WHITES**
To brighten whites that can't be bleached, just pour a small amount of lemon juice into the washing machine at the start of the wash cycle.

**INK STAINS**
To remove ink from fabric, apply lemon juice liberally while the ink is still wet. Then wash the garment with regular detergent in cold water.

**RASPBERRY AND RED CURRANT STAINS**
Dab the stain with lemon juice, rinse in warm water, and then wash in the normal way.

**RID CLOTHES OF MILDEW**
You unpack the clothes you've stored for the season and discover that some of the garments are stained with mildew. To get rid of mildew on clothes, make a paste of lemon juice and salt and rub it on the affected area, then dry the clothes in sunlight. Repeat the process until the stain is gone.

**RUST STAINS**
Rust stains can be removed by rubbing with a solution of lemon juice and salt. Let stand for a few hours and then wash as normal.

## STAINS ON WHITE CLOTHING

Make up a paste of cream of tartar and lemon juice and apply the mixture to the stain. Lay the clothing in the sun to soak, checking periodically to see if the stain has lifted. After soaking, wash the garment as normal.

## STUBBORN STAINS

Pour equal parts of white vinegar and lemon juice into a dish. Submerse the stain in the mixture and soak for 30 minutes to 1 hour. Wash as usual.

## WHITE SOCKS

To get really white socks, boil them in water with a slice of lemon.

## GENERAL GREEN CLEANING

AIR FRESHENER ........ 136
BRASS, COPPER, AND STAINLESS STEEL ........ 136
CEILING FAN ........ 136
CHROME ........ 136
FIREPLACE FUMES ........ 136
FURNITURE POLISH ........ 136
HUMIDIFIER ........ 137
MARBLE ........ 137
PIANO CLEANER ........ 137
VACUUM CLEANER ........ 137
WOODEN FLOOR CLEANER ........ 137

## AIR FRESHENER

If you want nice smelling rooms, try cutting a lemon in half and placing the 2 halves cut-side up in a dish on a windowsill. The air in your room will soon smell lemon fresh.

Alternatively, add sliced lemons and cinnamon to a pan of water and simmer for one hour.

## BRASS, COPPER, AND STAINLESS STEEL

To clean tarnished brass, copper, or stainless steel, make a paste of lemon juice and salt and coat the affected area. Let it stand for 5 minutes, then wash off with warm water. Buff with a dry, soft cloth. You can also use this paste to clean a stainless steel sink.

## CEILING FAN

To get rid of dust from a ceiling fan, clean it with an old sock and lemon juice. It is perfect for killing those dangerous microbes or spores that can otherwise circulate around the room.

## CHROME

Polish chrome by simply rubbing lemon rind over it and watch it shine. Rinse well and dry with a soft cloth.

## FIREPLACE FUMES

Next time you have a fire that sends horrible fumes into your room, try throwing a few pieces of lemon peel into the flames. Alternatively, you could burn some pieces of peel with your firewood as a preventive measure.

## FURNITURE POLISH

Make your own furniture polish. It is much better for wood than any proprietary brand, but only make a small amount at a time because you need to use it when it is fresh. Mix the juice of one lemon, one teaspoon of olive oil and a teaspoon of water. Apply a thin coat to furniture and buff to a deep shine.

**IUMIDIFIER**

o make a natural humidifier that makes the room smell ice at the same time, place an enameled cast-iron pot n top of your stove and fill with water. Add lemon peel, innamon sticks, cloves, and apple skins and allow to immer.

**ARBLE**

arble is very porous and, therefore, easily stained. Try utting a lemon in half, dipping the exposed flesh in some able salt, and then rub it vigorously on the stain. Make ure you rinse the surface well because acid can damage ne marble.

**IANO CLEANER**

ub a paste of 2 parts salt and 1 part lemon juice onto irty piano keys. Then wipe it off with a damp cloth, and uff the keys with a dry one.

**ACUUM CLEANER**

o freshen your vacuum cleaner, place a few drops of emon juice into the bag just before you start your hores.

**VOODEN FLOOR CLEANER**

o clean wooden floors that haven't been varnished, wash hem with a solution of lemon juice and water. Not only vill your room smell nice, but the floor will look amazing s well.

## PESTS AND PETS

FLEAS .......................................................... 13
INSECT BITES .................................................. 13
PET STAINS/ODOR ON CARPET.............................. 13

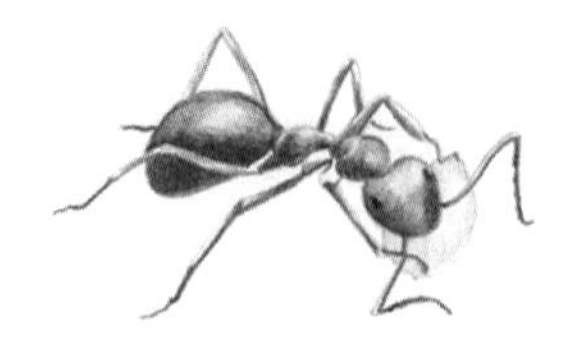

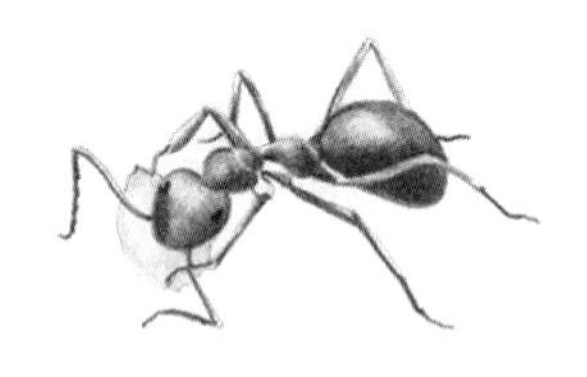

### FLEAS

If you want to keep fleas at bay, mix the juice of 4 lemons with ½ gallon (2 liters) of water and wash your floors with it. Watch the fleas hop away; they simply hat the smell of lemons.

### INSECT BITES

Dab a little lemon juice onto the infected area to help reduce swelling and stop the itching.

### PET STAINS/ODOR ON CARPET

To remove discoloration after pet messes are cleaned, apply a generous amount of lemon juice to the area and let it soak for 15 to 30 minutes. Reapply if needed. Once the stain is removed, rinse and blot dry.

You can also use a mixture of lemon juice and cream of tartar. As before, let it dry, rinse, and blot.

## MISCELLANEOUS GREEN USES

BLEACH ........................................................ 140
BLEMISHES .................................................... 140
COUGH SYRUP ................................................ 140
DANDRUFF .................................................... 140
DIGESTION .................................................... 140
DISINFECTANT ................................................ 140
FINGERNAILS ................................................... 141
FLOWER FRESHENER.......................................... 141
HEADACHE CURE .............................................. 141
INVISIBLE INK ................................................... 141
KEEP RICE FROM STICKING ................................ 141
LEATHER SHOE STAINS...................................... 141
LEMON ICE CUBES ........................................... 141
LIGHTEN HIGHLIGHTS ....................................... 142
POISON IVY ..................................................... 142
ROUGH SKIN .................................................... 142
SORE THROAT................................................... 142
STORING LEMONS ............................................ 142
VINEGAR.......................................................... 142
WEEDS ............................................................ 142

Apart from using lemons for cleaning, there are a variety of different uses—why don't you try them out for yourselves.

### BLEACH

To remove the smell of bleach from your hands and also to get rid of that horrible slimy feeling, simply pour lemon juice over your skin and then rinse. (Bleach is alkaline and lemon is acid, so they cancel each other out and balance the pH of your skin). This method also works well on removing the smell of onion or garlic from your hands.

### BLEMISHES

If you have unsightly blemishes on your face, mix the juice of one lemon with one tablespoon of honey and apply to clean skin. Let stand for a couple of minutes and then rinse. Your skin will be glowing and future blemishes will be greatly reduced.

### COUGH SYRUP

Mix 1 part lemon juice with 2 parts honey. (Do not give to children below the age of one year.)

### DANDRUFF

To cure dandruff, apply 1 tablespoon of lemon juice to your hair. Shampoo, then rinse with water. Rinse again with a mixture of 2 tablespoons of lemon juice and 2 cups (475 ml) of water. Repeat every other day until dandruff disappears.

### DIGESTION

To aid digestion, drink lemon juice with water in the morning or at any time throughout the day.

### DISINFECTANT

To stop bleeding and disinfect minor wounds, pour lemon juice on a cut or apply with a piece of cotton wool. Remember, though, it will sting!

**INGERNAILS**

whiten, brighten, and make your fingernails stronger, ak them in lemon juice for 10 minutes, then brush with mixture of equal parts white vinegar and warm water. inse well.

**LOWER FRESHENER**

keep your cut flowers looking fresh for longer mix tablespoon sugar with 2 tablespoons lemon juice and dd to the water each time you change it.

**EADACHE CURE**

cure a headache, drink a small cup of black coffee ixed with the juice of half a lemon. It tastes awful, but certainly does the job!

**VISIBLE INK**

you want to play at being a spy and write an invisible essage, use a cotton bud as a pen to write in lemon iice on a piece of white paper. Once it dries, hold the aper near a hot lightbulb (but remember DON'T TOUCH). ıst like magic the writing will turn brown.

**EEP RICE FROM STICKING**

keep your rice from sticking together in clumps, add a oonful of lemon juice to the boiling water when ooking. When the rice is done, let it cool for a few inutes, then fluff with a fork before serving.

**EATHER SHOE STAINS**

our lemon juice on a cloth, add cream of tartar, and assage into the shoe leather. When the stain has gone, nse and buff with a cloth.

**EMON ICE CUBES**

add lemon and ice to your drink in one easy step, put nall pieces of lemon into your ice trays and then add ater and freeze.

## LIGHTEN HIGHLIGHTS

To brighten those fading highlights, rinse your hair with 1 cup (225 ml) of lemon juice mixed with ¾ cup (175 ml) of water.

## POISON IVY

To soothe the itching and alleviate the rash, apply lemon juice to the areas that have been affected by coming int contact with poison ivy.

## ROUGH SKIN

To relieve rough skin on your hands or feet, apply lemon juice, rinse, and then massage the skin with olive oil.

## SORE THROAT

Drinking tea with lemon and honey helps to relax a sore throat, while also relieving a cough.

## STORING LEMONS

Store whole lemons in a jar of water in the refrigerator. They will yield a lot more juice this way.

## VINEGAR

If you don't like the smell of vinegar when used for cleaning, try adding some lemon juice as well and this will help neutralize the smell.

## WEEDS

If you want to get rid of those unsightly weeds growing up between your paving stones, simply douse them with lemon juice and watch them shrivel within a day or two.

# SALT

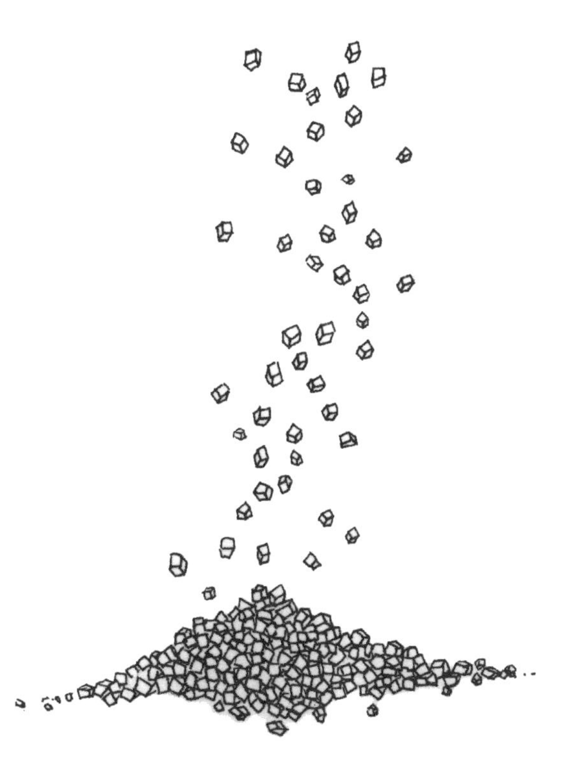

# SALT IN OUR LIVES

For many people, salt is just a white granular substance you sprinkle onto your food. However, do you realize that salt is actually a commodity that we cannot do without. Every species of living creature needs the sodium in salt, but through changes during evolution, social groupings, and civilization we now consume far more than we need. The salt on the table is just the tip of the iceberg. It is everywhere in our daily lives.

Its industrial uses are phenomenal. In fact, only a small percentage of the salt produced in the world is used for food preservation or seasoning. It may yet contribute in some way to renewable energy sources.

Historically, salt has been the cause of wars, uprisings, and revolutions. It has been taxed all over the world, used as money, and has been a powerful force in the economic rise and fall of civilizations. Religions, ceremonies, and rituals rely on salt. You can't really ignore it.

There are many ways in which salt can be used around the home. Don't just look upon salt as a seasoning that should be used sparingly. Here are just a few suggestions for helping with some tough domestic jobs. Many of these may look slightly familiar, especially if you have already read the section on baking soda.

# Green Cleaning Solutions with Salt

## GENERAL GREEN CLEANING USES

BATHTUB AND TOILET CLEANER ............................ 147
BLOODSTAINS .................................................. 147
CLEAN BRASS, COPPER, AND PEWTER .................... 147
CLEANING A COFFEEPOT OR JUG .......................... 147
CLEANING CLOTHS AND SPONGES .......................... 147
CLEANING PANS ............................................. 147
CLEANING THE PIANO ....................................... 147
CLOTHES LINES ............................................... 147
DISCOLORED GLASS ......................................... 148
DRAINS ......................................................... 148
GETTING RID OF SOAP SUDS ............................... 148
HANDKERCHIEF STAIN REMOVAL ........................... 148
INK STAINS .................................................. 148
METAL CLEANER ............................................. 148
MILDEW ......................................................... 148
MOPPING UP IN THE OVEN ................................. 148
NEW LAMPS FOR OLD ....................................... 149
PRESERVING BRUSHES ....................................... 149
PRESERVING CLOTHES PINS ................................. 149
REFRESHING WHITES ....................................... 149
REMOVING GREASE ......................................... 149
REMOVING INK FROM A CARPET .......................... 149
REMOVING RED WINE FROM A TABLECLOTH ............. 150
RINGS ON FURNITURE ....................................... 150
STOCKINGS OR PANTY HOSE ............................... 150
TO CLEAN AN IRON ......................................... 150
WICKER FURNITURE ......................................... 150

hese tips are passed on in good faith. If in doubt about leaning a particular item, please refer to expert advice.

**ATHTUB AND TOILET CLEANER**
ome people must have very grubby bathtubs, or very rubby bodies. Mixing salt with turpentine whitens your athtub and toilet bowl, apparently. Not recommended or smokers!

**LOODSTAINS**
losebleed? Cut finger? Soak clothing in a bucket of salty vater as soon as possible to prevent staining.

**CLEAN BRASS, COPPER, AND PEWTER**
Make a paste using salt and vinegar thickened with flour o clean your brass, copper, and pewter.

**CLEANING A COFFEEPOT OR JUG**
Jse salt to clean your discolored coffeepot or jug.

**CLEANING CLOTHS AND SPONGES**
reshen sponges and cloths by soaking them in salt water.

**CLEANING PANS**
oak enameled pans in salt water overnight and boil them vith salty water the next day to remove burned-on tains. Don't soak chipped pans or metal ones.

**CLEANING THE PIANO**
'm not brave enough to subject our ancient piano keys to his one, I'm afraid. Perhaps it is better for newer models ather than ivory. The suggestion is to mix lemon juice vith salt to clean the keys.

**CLOTHES LINES**
Soaking your clothes line in salt water will prevent your clothes from freezing to the line. Alternatively, use salt in

your final rinse to prevent the clothes from freezing. Better still, dry them indoors.

### DISCOLORED GLASS

Soak discolored glass in a salt-and-vinegar solution to remove stains.

### DRAINS

Remove odors from your sink drain pipe with a strong, hot solution of salt water.

### GETTING RID OF SOAP SUDS

Rinsing clothes with a little salt in the water can get rid of excess soap. This is also said to help fabrics to hold their color.

### HANDKERCHIEF STAIN REMOVAL

If you are the type who still prefers to use real handkerchiefs, especially when you have a cold (they don't seem to hurt tender areas when you have a very runny nose), soak them in salt water before washing. You can then rinse them before washing alongside other clothes in the washing machine.

### METAL CLEANER

Clean brass, copper, and pewter with a paste made from salt and vinegar, thickened with flour. Baking soda works better I think, and without the flour.

### MILDEW

A mixture of salt and lemon juice will remove mildew.

### MOPPING UP IN THE OVEN

If something bubbles over in your oven, put a handful of salt on top of the spilled juice. The mess won't smell and will bake into a dry, light crust, which you can wipe off easily when the oven has cooled.

ou can also sprinkle salt into milk-scorched pans to
emove the odor.

### IEW LAMPS FOR OLD

olish your old kerosene lamp with salt for a brighter
ook. You never know what genie you may find!

### RESERVING BRUSHES

oak new brushes in warm, salty water before you first
se them. They will apparently last longer.

### RESERVING CLOTHES PINS

oiling clothes pins in salt water before using them may
nake them last longer, apparently. They'll need careful
lrying, however.

### EFRESHING WHITES

estore yellowed cottons or linens to their original white
y boiling the items for one hour in a salt-and-baking
oda solution. Perspiration stains may be removed by
dding 4 tablespoons of salt to 4 cups (1 liter) of hot
vater. If you can't soak the item, sponge the fabric with
he solution until the stains disappear.

### EMOVING GREASE

o remove grease stains on clothing, mix one part salt to
our parts alcohol. If it works on the bathtub, it will work
n the clothes.

### EMOVING INK FROM A CARPET

o remove an ink spot from a carpet, pour salt onto the
tain and let it soak up the liquid before brushing up the
alt. As with all stain removals, try on an inconspicuous
art of carpet first.

### REMOVING RED WINE FROM A TABLECLOTH

Since you can't usually whip off the tablecloth if a guest
spills red wine on your best cloth, just pour a little salt

onto the splash immediately. This will soak up the wine, then you can soak the cloth at the end of the meal and brush up any salt that has escaped the cloth.

### RINGS ON FURNITURE

Remove white rings left on tables caused by wet or hot dishes and glasses. Rub a thin paste of vegetable oil and salt onto the spot and let the mixture stand for an hour or two before removing. As always, try out the technique first on a less conspicuous mark if possible. Complete the process by polishing the whole item of furniture.

### STOCKINGS OR PANTY HOSE

If you have odd stockings or panty hose of different colors, try boiling them in salty water and they will come out matched, and hopefully without holes.

### TO CLEAN AN IRON

Rub some salt onto a damp cloth and apply to a warm, but not hot, iron. Switch off the iron first, of course.

### WICKER FURNITURE

Rub any wicker furniture you may have with salt water to prevent yellowing.

## PEST PREVENTION

ANT DETERRENT .............................................. 150
REPEL FLEAS ................................................. 150
WEEDS AND SLUGS........................................... 150
WEED-FREE PATHS .......................................... 150

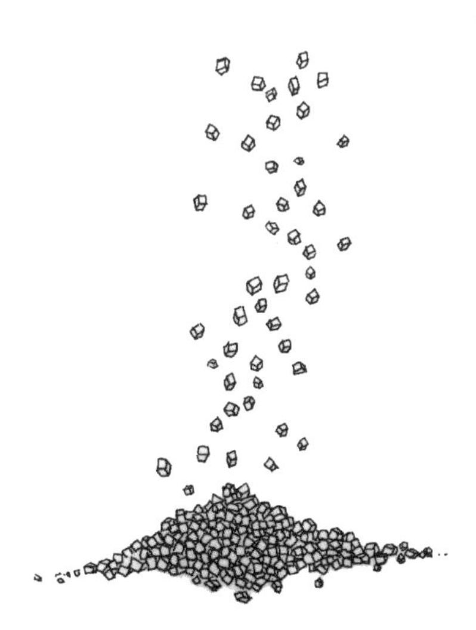

### ANT DETERRENT

Sprinkle salt onto your shelves to keep ants away. I don't recommend this where you may have any damp getting in, or where the salt is likely to spill onto a floor.

### REPEL FLEAS

Repel fleas by washing your dog's bed in salty water.

### WEEDS AND SLUGS

Use salt for killing weeds in your lawn or slugs and snails in the garden.

### WEED-FREE PATHS

Sprinkle salt between bricks or paving slabs where you don't want grass (or any other plants) to grow.

## MISCELLANEOUS GREEN USES

BRUSHING TEETH .......... 153
CANDLES .......... 153
CUTS AND SCRATCHES .......... 153
FLOWERS .......... 153
POISON IVY .......... 153
REMOVING A SPLINTER .......... 153
SETTING A COLOR .......... 153
SOOTHE A BEE STING .......... 153
SORE MOUTHS/GARGLE .......... 154
TESTING EGGS .......... 154
VASES .......... 154
WINDOWS .......... 154

**BRUSHING TEETH**

Use equal parts of salt and baking soda for brushing your teeth. Dry salt sprinkled on your toothbrush makes a good tooth polisher. Ouch!

**CANDLES**

Soak new candles in a strong salt solution for a few hours and then dry to reduce dripping wax.

**CUTS AND SCRATCHES**

A mild salt solution is a good way to clean small cuts and scratches, using the antibacterial qualities of salt.

**FLOWERS**

Add a pinch of salt to the water in the vase your cut flowers will stand in. They will last longer.

**POISON IVY**

Kill poison ivy by adding 3 pounds (1.4 kg) of salt to 1 gallon (3.75 liters) of soapy water and spray it onto the leaves and stems.

**REMOVING A SPLINTER**

To remove a splinter from a finger easily, soak the area in warm salty water for a few minutes. If this doesn't work, mix a little water with half a teaspoon of baking soda to form a paste. Apply this to a splinter and cover it with a bandaid for a couple of hours. The soda should draw out the splinter, which can then be easily removed, along with any toxins, and solve the problem.

**SETTING A COLOR**

If a dye runs, soak the garment for an hour in 2 quarts (2 liters) of water to which you have added 2 tablespoons of vinegar and a 1 tablespoon of salt. If the rinse water still shows the color, repeat.

**SOOTHE A BEE STING**

Wet the sting right away, then cover it with salt.

## SORE MOUTHS/GARGLE

Mild salt water makes an effective mouthwash. Use it hot for a sore throat gargle.

## TESTING EGGS

To test for the freshness of eggs, put them in a bowl of salt water. Fresh eggs sink—bad ones float!

## VASES

Clean the dirt and nasty smell out of vases after the flowers are dead by rubbing the inside with salt water.

## WINDOWS

To keep single-glazed windows from freezing outside, rub the inside of the window with a sponge dipped in a salt water solution and wipe dry.

# OTHER GREEN ALTERNATIVES

# TEA TREE OIL

You have probably seen it in a list of ingredients in a shampoo or skin cream, but do you really know the full value of tea tree oil? The Aborigines of Australia have known about its valuable properties for a very long time. They have used it to treat wounds and infections, bathed in it, and even drunk it. Tea tree oil has been proven to be a powerful yet natural antiviral, antibacterial, and antifungal medicine, and these benefits can be used in your home as well.

The essential oil comes from the *Melaleuca alternifolia* tree, which has needlelike leaves. A word of caution though, tea tree oil is very pungent and potent. It should only be used externally, and sparingly. It should be kept away from babies or small children. Keep it away from your eyes and wash your hands after using it.

Tea tree oil is a natural solvent and when added to cleaning products from laundry detergent to bathroom cleaners, it helps cut through grease and stains effectively while killing germs and bacteria.

Listed here are just a few of the uses of tea tree oil in an effort to make your home a greener place:

## BASIC TEA TREE OIL SOLUTION

Put 2 teaspoons of tea tree oil into a spray bottle containing 1 pint (475 ml) of water.

## DEODORIZER

Spray the above formula into the air to deodorize a room.

## DISHWASHERS

Add a few drops of tea tree oil to your dishwasher dispenser and then add your normal detergent. This will help remove the residue built up on your dishes.

**GROUT CLEANING**

Use the above formula to spray grout. This will repel mold and mildew and although it will not take away all the discoloration caused by the mold, it will certainly kill it off.

**HOUSEHOLD ANTISEPTIC SPRAY**

Use the above formula to spray areas that need disinfecting.

**HUMIDIFIER**

Add a few drops of tea tree oil to your humidifier. This will clean, disinfect, and refresh the air.

**INSECT REPELLANT**

Wash your kitchen floor using water and a few drops of tea tree oil because it makes a wonderful insect repellant. It not only keeps those unwanted pests away but it also gives the washed area that just cleaned smell. Use it to wash your kitchen cabinets and work surfaces as well.

**LAUNDRY**

Add a few drops of tea tree oil to your laundry. This will disinfect and leave the laundry smelling clean and fresh.

**MUSTY MOLD REMOVER**

Spray the above formula onto mold but do not rinse.

# BORAX

Borax is probably best known as a laundry booster because it helps make the water soft and also leaves your clothes cleaner and brighter. Borax, or sodium borate, is a natural alkaline mineral that was first discovered 4000 years ago and has been used for cleaning and deodorizing for many years. It is a nonabrasive white powder that has no toxic fumes, making it safe for the environment. You can buy borax in most stores where you would buy your normal laundry detergent.

## GREEN CLEANING WITH BORAX

### ALL-PURPOSE CLEANER

Put 2 teaspoons of borax in a spray bottle with 2 cups (475 ml) of very hot water and shake to blend.

### ALUMINUM

Borax is safe to use on aluminum because it is nonabrasive, so sprinkle the powder onto your pans and rub with a cloth. Rinse items thoroughly.

### EXTRACTOR HOODS

To help get rid of grease and odors, mix a strong solution of soda crystals and/or borax in the sink and let the filter soak for 15 minutes before rinsing.

### DEODORIZING RERIGERATORS AND MICROWAVES

Borax is excellent for cleaning both your refrigerator and your microwave. Spilled food can be simply washed away using a soft cloth dipping in a solution of borax and hot water (1 tablespoon borax to 4 cups/1 liter of water).

### DISHWASHER

Make your own dishwasher powder by mixing a tablespoon of borax with a tablespoon of baking soda.

### FINE CHINA

Fine china will have a brilliant shine if you rinse it in a solution of borax and warm water, even hand-painted designs will not fade using this method. Make sure you rinse well with clear water.

### FLEAS

Sprinkle borax on dog beds, carpets, and other areas where you suspect that fleas could be lurking. Borax releases boric acid, which is poisonous to the fleas.

### FLOOR AND WALL CLEANER

Mix together 1 gallon (3.75 liters) of warm water with 6 tablespoons of borax and a teaspoon of liquid soap. Use to mop floors or clean walls.

### GROUT CLEANER

Mix together 2 tablespoons of baking soda, 1 tablespoon of borax, and enough water to form a thin paste. Apply to the grout, scrub, and rinse.

### MICE DETERRENT

Sprinkle borax on the floor around the sides of the walls. Mice do not like getting borax on their feet, so they are less likely to return to that area of the house.

### MOLD INHIBITOR

Make up a thick paste using borax and water and smear it onto the moldy area. Let it dry overnight, then sweep up the powder and rinse. You do not need to worry about your paintwork being damaged.

### DIAPERS

Rinse out diapers and begin soaking immediately, using 6 tablespoons of borax for each bucket of warm water. Follow soaking with a warm machine wash and add a small amount of white vinegar instead of fabric conditioner to produce a soft and absorbent fabric.

## SCOURING POWDER

Mix together a tablespoon each of borax, baking soda, and salt to make an excellent scouring powder.

## TOILET BOWL

Pour some borax into the toilet bowl before going to bed and the following morning clean with a brush. You will find the job becomes effortless because the borax has loosened any buildup of grime.

## WASHING DISHES

Instead of using dish-washing detergent, use a tablespoon of borax in a sinkful of water. If your dishes are very greasy, it is worth adding a little dish-washing detergent as well.

## WASTE DISPOSAL UNITS AND DRAINS

Borax helps deodorize waste disposal units by neutralizing acidic odors. Sprinkle 2–3 tablespoons in the drain, let it stand for 15 minutes, and then flush with clean water for a few seconds.